WHERE IS GOD IN HIS CHURCH?

John Wallace Whitehead

WESTBOW
PRESS
A DIVISION OF THOMAS NELSON

WestBow Press books may be ordered through booksellers or by contacting:

WestBow Press
A Division of Thomas Nelson
1663 Liberty Drive
Bloomington, IN 47403
www.westbowpress.com
1-(866) 928-1240

Because of the dynamic nature of the Internet, any web addresses or links contained in this book may have changed since publication and may no longer be valid. The views expressed in this work are solely those of the author and do not necessarily reflect the views of the publisher, and the publisher hereby disclaims any responsibility for them.

Any people depicted in stock imagery provided by Thinkstock are models, and such images are being used for illustrative purposes only.

Certain stock imagery © Thinkstock.

ISBN: 978-1-4497-1868-8 (sc)
ISBN: 978-1-4497-1869-5 (hc)
ISBN: 978-1-4497-1867-1 (e)

Library of Congress Control Number: 2011930622

Printed in the United States of America

WestBow Press rev. date: 07/27/2011

This book is dedicated to my family, who has encouraged me to be more than I could be and seen in me more than I am.

To my mom, Ann Bridges, who has since passed away but has never left me and who always saw more in me than there really was. I miss you, Mom, and will see you again someday.

To my wife, Bonnie, who shares her life with me and who sees me as I really am and loves me anyway. Thank you, Bonnie. I will always love you.

To my daughter, Lindsay, who believes I can be so much more than I am, I am very proud of you and the woman you have become.

And to my son, John, who talks with me and challenges me to consider the things in life that are often overlooked and many times misunderstood. Thank you, John.

It is because of the Lord Jesus Christ, who tells Peter and us in Matthew 16:18, "And I tell you that you are Peter, and on this rock I will build my church, and the gates of Hades will not overcome it," that I know God is continuing to build His Church, and my purpose for writing this is dedicated to that belief.

There is now, nor has there ever been, a greater instrument that has been used by God to reach mankind with the Gospel than His Church, the Body of Christ.

We who believe and call on the name of Jesus as Lord and Savior are that "Body."

We are that Church.

A Special Thank You

I want to give a special thank you to Dr. Gregory Strayer, Professor of English at Trinity College of Florida, for the initial editing of this book. As I tried to communicate throughout this book, I am a work in progress.

I also thank Dr. Mark O'Farrell, President of Trinity College of Florida, for encouragement throughout this process.

CONTENTS

Foreword by David Lane

David Lane is the Senior Pastor of Edgewater Alliance Church in Edgewater, FL, a Christian and Missionary Alliance Church of approximately 600. He is also the Moderator for the CMA's Southeastern District's Licensing, Ordination and Consecration Council (LOCC).

There are times in life when we need a wake-up call. Maybe we've grown slack in our diet, sending our cholesterol through the roof, and a blood test is the wake-up call we need. Blood tests are always better than heart attacks when it comes to sounding the alarm that we are in trouble. If we are in trouble, we want something or someone to sound the alarm to alert us. The Church in America is in trouble, and John Whitehead has dared to ask the question that should serve as the Church's wake-up call.

Where is God in His Church?

When I began reading this book, I thought I was reading to review it. However, I soon found that the nature of this book led me to review me. John's love for Jesus and His Bride, the Church, was always evident throughout our friendship, and that love remains evident in his writing. This book is written to serve the Church rather than tear it down. The pages moved me to assess my life and the ways I may be attempting to push God out of His Church. Beyond articulating the obvious problems the Church has, John challenges his readers to ask the hard questions that need to be asked in order to sound the alarm.

Anyone who knows John knows he is a man of action. While many of us are content to talk about problems, John is always ahead, doing something to solve those problems. He wrote this book to stir the Church to action. We must begin with what Jim Collins, in his book *Good to Great,* calls, "confronting the brutal facts." The brutal fact is we may have pushed God out of our church with our misguided desire to protect Him. The brutal fact is we may have reinforced the world's observation that God isn't in our churches through our temple-minded theology.

John has taken action by providing this book, this blood test, so that the Church in America can avoid the spiritual heart attack that follows the discovery that God has left *our* church. Thank you, John, for reminding us that it is His Church and Jesus Christ is Her Head.

—David Lane

INTRODUCTION

As I sit and once again begin to write this book, if that is what it becomes, I have come to the conclusion that I am writing this as much for myself as for anyone who might read it. I have spent a considerable amount of time recently, trying to collect my thoughts and praying (though certainly not praying as much as I should have) about what I am doing with my life. What are my priorities? Where does ministry and God Himself rate in my life? What am I doing to help further God's kingdom here on earth?

I think, for me as for most, the questions that continually pop up are ones that start with me. Am I effective in my witness for Jesus? Is my life Christ-centered and Christ-focused? As a part of the Body of Christ, am I following His example, or have I created my own paradigm? Like many men my age and in situations similar to mine, if I had just recently bought a sports car or a big boat, I would think I was having a midlife crisis. In fact, I have sold both of these things in the last few years (although the boat wasn't big).

At this moment, I feel that if there is a crisis in my life, it is one of self-awareness, and it is a self-awareness that is focusing in on the spiritual aspects of my life, not on the physical or material, and for this I am eternally grateful. This must be the Lord, because I am all too aware of my own abilities to be self-absorbed and self-focused, and I am all too sure of my own self- importance in my life.

As I move forward, I sincerely hope to explore and address some of these issues that create many of the questions I, as well as many others I know, have about our relationship with Jesus and where He is in *His Church*.

By that, I mean where have I, or we, placed Him? If He is not the focus of our attention, then, as an individual and as a "Body," we are sick and may quite possibly be in danger of dying. I am sure this sounds harsh to many, but this is a reality we face in our culture today. The evidence that supports my contention can be seen most clearly in the decline of the Church in America and the decline or stagnation of most of our churches.

As I consider writing these thoughts, I am certain it is equally as important I ask myself my reasons for doing so. The question I am asking of myself at this point is one I have asked others when I have been involved in counseling sessions or meetings requested by someone to express a view or an opinion about something they see or perceive as a problem.

Whether it is in their personal lives, in someone else's life, or in the Church itself, the question always cuts to the heart of the matter for me. Is my reason for bringing this up an effort to be constructive, or am I just being critical? This is a question we all should be asking ourselves when trying to communicate a differing view or an observation of a situation or circumstance we have experienced or are experiencing.

Although we may believe we are being constructive, we need—and in this case, I need—to be sure it is not out of a desire to cast stones or a need to vindicate ourselves (myself) for past hurts or perceived offenses. Rather, it should be out of a genuine desire to bring to the forefront an area of concern that needs to be addressed. If we can honestly say we believe this is true and that our focus is Jesus and His "Mission" when we ask these types of questions, we should go ahead and, as Paul stated in 1 Thessalonians 5:21HCSB, "but test all things. Hold on to what is good"

In this case, I can honestly say I truly believe it is in an effort to be and my intention to be constructive. I am certain you and I could, in our experiences both in the church and in everyday life, find a lot of reasons to be critical. I am also sure many people could find many reasons to be critical of each of us. But if we can begin again to, "Test everything," perhaps we will be able to see the need for constructive criticism in our personal lives and in the Church.

There truly is need, although it is rarely the case we should desire the pursuit and the application of such criticism.

I would like to begin by giving you some personal background information that may help anyone reading this to understand or perhaps, if people so choose, to come up with a conclusion of their own about my perceptions. At the least, they should be able to develop a basic understanding of them.

Throughout this book, I attempt to share my view in a way I hope is truthful and thoughtful but, hopefully, devoid of representing the same attitudes and biases I believe are present in the Church today and against which I am about to speak.

As I begin to write this for others to see and read, my hope and prayer is that the Lord will use this time as a time of personal introspection for me and that those who read it consider their own views and perspectives and give thought to the question, Where is God in His Church?

My desired end result for writing this book is personal spiritual growth. Hopefully, writing this will help me better understand myself and my relationship with the Lord as I consider His Church. My heartfelt desire is that at the very least, this will give me and each of us food for thought, as we travel along this journey He has so graciously allowed us to travel.

He, who is the source of all, is in all, above all, and over all.

A Changed Life

My Childhood

I have been a Christian for the better part of forty-one years. I was born in Charlotte, North Carolina, in 1959. Our family moved to West Palm Beach, Florida, in 1967 when I was about eight or nine years old.

When I think about my childhood, I see my family as being pretty typical of other families I knew or at least typical of what I understood a family to be. Although my mother always provided for us and did the best she could, the greatest lesson that I learned from her was how to love. She taught my brothers and my sister and me to do this by demonstrating love to us—not just with words, but with genuine affection. We are a hugging, kissing, touching people; and though these actions may make others uncomfortable at times, they are how we learned to demonstrate our love for each other.

As I consider my mother's love and affection, I believe showing them to my siblings and me was her way of giving us what she could because while we were young her love was all she had to give us.

Although her example to us was not one focused on the Lord, we were not unlike most families I knew of at that time. Our family did not spend time praying or reading God's Word. However, if we had been asked, I am certain that each of us would have said we believed in Jesus.

My mom (Sylvia Ann Bridges) was seventeen years old when I was born. By the time we moved to Florida, she was a twenty-five-year-old single mother with three children. As I said, she always did the best she could for us on her own. She was strict and had no problem using the rod or the brush or ruler or belt or whatever she could get her hands on at the time. Her methods would probably be considered extreme by today's standards, but I don't think they did us any harm. I know that this punishment didn't do me any harm.

My mother was bright, cheery, and full of life; and at the same time, she could be as strong and as tough as anyone I have ever met. She stood five feet tall in heels. and was afraid of nothing. For those of us who knew her, that attitude and tenacity gave you the impression that she thought she was six feet tall and bullet proof .When my mom was there, she was the center of the action, and we loved her for it.

I loved my mother with all my heart. I watched her struggle to make ends meet. Although we never had the material wealth that my children now enjoy, I can honestly say I never remember doing without.

Because I was the oldest child, my mother was also my friend and would confide in me about many of her struggles in life.

This situation wasn't always comfortable for me, and I probably wasn't always capable of dealing with that aspect of our relationship. But I don't regret it in the least.

She was a source of strength and encouragement for me throughout my life, and I love her for that.

Along with my wife, my mom was my biggest fan. She truly believed that I was capable of doing and being so much more than I thought I could. But I appreciated her unwavering love and belief in me.

One of the issues that I will bring out in this book is the idea of "perception being reality."

Although we received food and housing from the State of North Carolina prior to our moving to Florida. I can honestly say that I never perceived us as economically challenged (that's politically correct for "poor")

This became apparent to me when I was in the fifth grade. During one basketball season, we couldn't afford my team uniform, so we dyed a T-shirt and wrote a number on it so I could play basketball. .

It was then that my reality revealed itself. The biggest challenge was dealing with the other kids, but I can honestly say no permanent damage was done. Again, that is my perception. People who truly know me may say differently, if asked.

It was shortly after moving to Florida that my mom met and married a man named Lester O'Neil Whitehead. He adopted the three of us and became our dad. He taught me how to hunt and fish, and he basically forced my mom to let my brother David and me become boys.

My relationship with him was estranged from about the age of fifteen until about three years before his death in 2005. My dad was an alcoholic, and that addiction cost him everything. But he was one of those people who never had a bad thing to say about anyone. He was one of the nicest people I have ever known. His demeanor was laid back, and his humor was dry. And when he laughed, he really laughed.

I spent a lot of time talking with him before his passing about six years ago now. It was by the grace of God that I was able to talk with him about life and about Jesus. About a year before his death, he was in the hospital near my home going through his second bout of chemotherapy for non-Hodgkin's lymphoma. I visited him there every day, and we spent a lot of time talking. He had a great heart, evidenced by his willingness to marry a woman and adopt her three children. I believe he died knowing the love of his children and of his Lord.

One thing that has always amazed me (and I will always remember about my dad) is that no matter how much time passed between our conversations, we never ran out of things to talk about. I can still hear how he would answer his phone if I called; or when I answered if he called me, he would say, "Well, hello there, Mr.

Whitehead." It would always bring a smile to my face. It does so now as I think about it. I miss hearing his greeting.

I realize now that God—in His infinite wisdom—used even my dad's death to bring glory to Himself. It was on the night my father passed away that my youngest brother, Bryan, accepted the Lord.

My dad was in an ICU in Tallahassee, Florida, after getting sepsis from brackish water. He had fallen through an old dock into the water and scraped his arm. Ironically, it wasn't the non-Hodgkin's lymphoma he had battled for the better part of three years that would cost him his life. Instead, it was fishing (my Dad could catch a fish in a mud puddle)—the thing my dad loved most—that ended his life.

While Dad was in the ICU, Bryan and I left the hospital to get some food and rest. In the hotel room, we were talking about Dad and life in general, and Bryan told me that one day he wanted to receive the Lord. I remember telling him, "Well, when you are ready to do that, I would be glad and honored to help you."

He looked and me and said, "Now seems like a pretty good time."

At the very moment that he received Jesus, the phone rang. It was my sister Lisa. Our dad had gone code blue. Bryan and I rushed back to the hospital. When we got there, the four of us (David, Lisa, Bryan, and I) went into the hospital chapel and prayed for direction. We decided to remove our dad from the life support machines. He died peacefully within minutes.

My brothers and my sister and I were all there when he died. I think it is the only time we had ever been together, just the four of us as adults. The only time we have been together since then was at the death of my mother, when she was in the ICU of a hospital in Jupiter, Florida.

My mother died in 2008, of something they called TTP - Thrombotic thrombocytopenic purpura, a blood disorder that causes blood clots to form in small blood vessels around the body, and leads to a low platelet count. She was diagnosed after being admitted to the hospital for tests. Losing her was the most devastating event that has ever occurred in my life thus far. I have already said that she was my source of love and encouragement. She believed that I could do no wrong. Oh, how blind love is! I believe many of the things I have been able to accomplish have happened directly as a result of my mother's belief in me. Her passing is still fresh and tender in my heart, and I suspect it always will be.

Today, in the center of my desk in my office, I have a crystal that my mom gave me. The inscription on the crystal reads," What you dare to dream, dare to do."

Those inspirational words are just an example to me of the way she was always able to motivate me to be more than I could ever dream I could be.

Fortunately, I did get to spend a considerable amount of time with her. Over the last two years of her life, I spent almost every Friday morning having coffee at her house.

I thank the Lord for prompting me to spend time with my mom. We spent those Friday mornings talking about Jesus and solving all the world's problems. We talked about anything and everything. Her Southern charm, wit, and style never wavered, and her ability to see the simplicity in life was truly amazing.

The one thing I can say with all certainty about my mother is that she left a legacy of love. I always knew that she loved me, and I hope and believe that she knew how much I loved her.

My mother is sorely missed, and the hole she left here in my world can never be filled. Although she did not spend her time teaching us about Jesus or making sure we were involved in church, she demonstrated love for my brothers, my sister, and me her entire life. I believe the ability to do that can only come from Him, and I look forward to seeing her again one day!

One of the last things she did was to introduce me to one of the nurses at the hospital. Her words gave credence to the Lord's call on my life: "This is my son Johnny. He's a minister." Thanks, Mom. I love you.

ACCEPTING JESUS

As for my spiritual life, regular Sunday morning church attendance was rare for us. As with many families we knew, we went to church on Easter Sunday and attended things like vacation Bible school or an occasional ministry of a nearby church that might be available such as Awana or Sunday school. It was on one of those rare events that I accepted the Lord. It was an Awana meeting at a Baptist church in West Palm Beach, Florida, when I was about ten years old.

I remember the experience clearly. As with many people I have talked with about the day they accepted the Lord, I don't remember experiencing any significant life change, and I did not consider my relationship with Jesus something that was alive, active, or growing until I was well into my twenties.

That being said, I do believe the Lord was working in my life all the while. Unfortunately, I was just like a lot of people. I overlooked God, as I enjoyed my life; I was not listening to anyone, especially Him. My teenage years were filled with every activity I could find to occupy myself and keep me out of the house (there was a time when kids went outside the house). But in all those activities, I have to admit that seeking a relationship with Jesus was not high on my list of things to do. In fact, if I am perfectly honest, He wasn't even a consideration most of the time.

I quit school in the eleventh grade, took my GED, and joined the US Navy. There I continued to grow in my pursuit of the pleasures of this life, and if I ever even thought about Jesus or my faith, it was when I felt it would benefit me somehow. It was only in certain situations, like when it got me out of work or out of standing a watch by going to church, that I became a Christian. I guess you could say I was, like many others, a Christian of convenience.

It was in my early twenties, after I had gotten out of the navy and married my wife, Bonnie (whom I had met at age fifteen), and with her and in many ways because of her, that I started attending church. It was there that I began to feel the call of God on my life. I responded by being baptized at age twenty-one. Again, no significant difference occurred in how I lived my life. I just had a greater sense of knowing I wasn't living the way I should.

A year later, we had a baby girl, Lindsay, and less than two years after that, we moved to a new home. It was there that we began attending a new church, and for the first time I can remember, I began to enjoy going to church. I actually looked forward to it.

The people seemed real and regular, the messages were pointed and applicable, and the music was Spirit-filled, worshipful, and well done. For the first time in my life, my desire to know more about God and His Word was growing. But I wasn't quite ready to grow—or at least to do the things I needed to do to grow.

We were pretty casual in our attendance. What I mean by that is we attended regularly (more than twice a month), but we were not really involved in the church.

The church entered into a building fund drive (something I will discuss more a little later), and as is the case with many such endeavors, things did not go well. We decided to find another place to attend services.

Answering the Call (Sort Of)

After leaving the church, a friend, Caspar McCloud, invited us to attend a church that was meeting in the little theater of a local high school. On our first visit, we found this church to be different than any with which we had ever been involved. It was filled with young, gifted people who were, by all indications, filled with love for God and for each other.

We started attending regularly, and for the first time in my life, I even began to seek ways to serve in a church. I helped set up and worked with the lighting equipment at the church during the two services it had each Sunday.

The reason I titled this segment "Answering the Call (Sort Of)" is because I was serving, but I was really still uncommitted. Although it had certainly improved, I was still casual about my attendance and still enjoying the lifestyle I had always enjoyed. I really liked what I was doing at the church, but I liked my life outside of church even more. And as with most of us, what I enjoyed most was what was relevant to me and where I placed my priorities.

I even remember telling the pastor's wife one Sunday that I would be leaving before the second service on any Sunday the Dolphins played at home, because I had season tickets and had to go. I told her I knew the Lord would understand, because He was a Dolphin fan. Until now, I never even considered how that probably

11

sounded, because, quite frankly at the time, it didn't matter to me. I am sure my brashness and directness about it were unsettling to her, but that is the way it was. It was as it had always been: "about me" and what I wanted to do. If I am perfectly honest, at that point in my life, that was all that mattered. Not my wife, not my kids, and certainly not my Lord.

Then, the God who patiently waits for each of us overwhelmed me with the realization of not only who He was but how much I needed Him if I was going to become the man He wanted me to be.

The Call Gets Louder

It was a Sunday morning in 1995 that they showed a video at church. Since I was doing the lights, I guess I showed it. It was a video about the Promise Keepers, a men's ministry that had just started. They showed a stadium filled with men in Denver, Colorado, who were crying and hugging. It was definitely not my cup of tea, and I honestly didn't have any real interest in it.

Later, I would understand that God had another plan. As it turned out, the church was having a meeting the next week for men who might be interested in going. To this day, I have no other explanation as to why I went, except the Holy Spirit moved me to go.

The guys there seemed all right, although I did not know any of them other than having possibly greeted them on Sunday morning. During that meeting, I met Gary Howell, and he asked me if I was going. I told him I was thinking about it but wasn't sure. He said he was going and I should go, too. We were as different as night and day, but there was something about him that I liked, and I decided to go.

As I look back now, I realize going to that meeting was a decision that truly changed my life, like no other experience ever had.

It was at this 1995 Promise Keepers' rally in Tampa, Florida, that I experienced what I would later come to understand was my "crisis of sanctification." It was there the Holy Spirit revealed Himself to me as He had never before. He did so by showing me how I was living my life. I knew the drinking and drugs were not what I should be doing, but that was how I lived my life and the way I had wanted to live it for as long as I could remember. To that point, every choice I made and considered was always weighed by what I wanted to do and what I enjoyed doing.

My wife, my children (by now I had a son, John, as well as my daughter, Lindsay), and my faith weren't enough to make me want to give up what I enjoyed. Besides, my attitude was probably not much different than most men's: I worked hard, I wasn't hurting anyone, and I deserved to do what I enjoyed. If there were going to be any growing taking place, it was going to be on my terms.

But as it is when the Lord speaks to us, He spoke directly to my heart—that cold, calloused, selfish place where I was hiding from Him. Please don't misunderstand me when I say He spoke to me. I did not hear an audible voice, but as many of you may attest, He spoke to me nevertheless. He reminded me I could not continue living my life as I was: living it my way, doing my thing, and making choices that were detrimental to me and to my young family.

In direct contrast to the world and the idea of making it on our own, the Lord reminded me I was not making it on my own and needed to realize it.

It was not the choice to be independent that was going to rescue me from myself. It was that choice to be dependent—dependent on Him—that was going to save me from myself.

It was crushing for me as a man, husband, and father when the speaker at the conference (I'm sorry I don't remember his name) stated that day, "You are the example of Jesus Christ to your children, just as He was the example of His Father to you."

I knew right then and there that I was going to have to change the way I was living, and that change had to start with learning to or being willing to rely on Him and not myself. It meant making changes: changes in my lifestyle and changes in my priorities. It was prompted by God through His Holy Spirit, and it occurred in His time, in my life.

It was at that moment that I started to do a survey of my life, kind of like an internal audit. What was I doing? My life had changed; I had grown up and become a man with responsibilities. Yet I was still involved in the same things I was doing when I was a kid. Yes, I was attending church. I was even at a men's rally with fifty-two thousand other men who professed, as I did, to being a "Christ follower." But the truth I discovered was that my life was not Christ centered: I was my priority. I had always been my priority—not God or my family. Doing what I wanted to do was all that really mattered to me. It was a sad revelation.

Even sadder was the understanding that I had been blessed with a wife and two young children, who were counting on me and trusting me to provide for them. I also realized I had an even more patient, understanding, and forgiving God, who had been waiting a long time for me to listen to His voice.

It was time to make a change. I knew it, and now I had to do it.

It had to start with giving up indulgences I had enjoyed since my teenage years. It was the only way I could begin even to consider living a life that would in some way exemplify Christ to my family. For me, this was a mountaintop experience. I knew to do this would cost me friends and interests that had long been a part of my life. I also knew it would be very difficult for me and would take time.

After finding my way clear to submit myself to the Lord's prompting, I began to look for ways to serve Him. Perhaps unbeknown to me, He was providing these opportunities to fill the voids that were left in my life from the changes that had begun to occur.

The first, and maybe the most significant, step was joining a small group. Most people I have talked with about small groups always come back with the same thoughts: I don't have time. I don't like all the sharing, and, I don't want to read or pray out loud. I understand all those issues and share and agree with many of them.

However, it is in a small group that most of us find significant spiritual growth. My advice to anyone who hasn't tried it is to take a risk, and see what God can do. In my case, several of us who met at the rally in Tampa began to meet together weekly at each other's homes. We began to study God's Word together, to pray for each other, and to hold each other accountable. It wasn't at all what I expected. It was actually a really good experience.

The group was a cross section of people from different areas and different backgrounds. Yet we all had one thing in common, the one thing that matters most: our faith in Jesus and our desire to learn more about ourselves as we learned more about Him.

We were growing, learning, and enjoying this newly found freedom in Christ. We were learning to become transparent and vulnerable. For many of us, certainly for me, this was the first time in our lives we had allowed anyone else to be a part of our struggles or even to admit we had them. We began to realize we were not alone in our struggles. Even people I thought had it all together were struggling with many of the same issues with which I struggled.

In the middle of this major growth process taking place in the lives of so many, this church, the one the Lord had led us to and the one He had used to bring about this monumental change in my life, developed a major issue, as happens in many churches.

This one was more devastating than a building fund. It concerned the pastor and his wife, and it caused division and confusion. Ultimately, it would tear apart the church. Even in the midst of all this goodness and growth, relationally and spiritually, problems developed, and things changed. It was the hardest decision I had made to this point in my life, but I felt led to leave, and I was not going to ignore the Spirit again. So after five years of attending, serving, and finally of growing, I had to lead my family to find a new place to worship.

I don't know how many of you have gone through this process. I am sure most of you have. But for me, it was miserable. What Bonnie and I discovered was that our lives revolved around our church and the people we had met there. Our friends and hearts were there.

We knew we had to find something to fill this void, so we spent the next several weeks church hopping. What we found was that we liked something over here, and we didn't like something over there. I am sure most of you have been there. We missed the people we had worshipped with for five years, and nothing seemed to fill that void.

As with the analogy of the "Body," it was as if we had been cut off from it. If you have been through this type of experience, you know that when you have been involved in a church in the context of a fellowship and you leave, nothing seems right.

The void that is left is reminiscent of losing a loved one, giving clear evidence of God's Word referencing the church as the Body. We had become a part of a community—a fellowship—and now we were not.

When you leave a church like this, you leave behind a little part of yourself. It is as if you lose a body part. It hurts, and it takes time for that pain to go away.

AN UNLIKELY PLACE

After looking around, we ended up in what I have to call a Podunk little church not too far from our house. There, our lives were forever impacted.

Through business, a man named Fred Harrington (who has since passed away) invited me to his church. It was west of our home and had a pole barn in front of it. It was so strange looking to me. In fact, I even called Fred after driving by it and asked him what kind of church it was. Truthfully, I wanted to make sure they weren't messing with snakes or anything like that. I will never forget his response. He said, "We are just a Bible-believing church."

With that understanding and a bit of uncertainty, we and another couple who had left our former church went to this small, unassuming church one Sunday morning.

I have to say it was at that point my life was forever changed. It was there I would meet a man named David Lane, who was about fourteen years younger than me. He was the youth pastor and would go on to become my best friend; he still is to this day.

Although I wasn't overly impressed the first Sunday we went, for some reason we decided to go back. And when we did, something happened that really had an impression on me. This youth pastor remembered my name. It may sound strange, but that blew me away. The pastor at the church we had left knew my name, but he never used it and always referred to me as "hotshot." I never did quite get that one.

It was in this small, unsophisticated church, with its grandfatherly pastor named Howard Dunlap, a young youth pastor, and barely tolerable music that I began to answer God's calling on my life. At first, I was guarded and certainly skeptical of this place and these people, but David Lane was for real. You could just see it. It was appealing, and in many ways, it was contagious.

David was living out his faith by serving where the Lord had called him. He, his wife, and their baby girl lived in a broken-down trailer provided by the church. He was gifted and certainly could have served in any number of larger churches, yet here he was, being used by God if, for no other reason, than to show me how to live a better life. His example has been the one I have appreciated most in my life and one I have hoped to model. What has always impressed me most about Dave is that, devoted though he was and is to his faith, he is very much a regular guy. This disarmed me and helped me see there was hope for a "wretch" like me.

I truly believe it is because of the Lord placing this man in my life that I began increasing my service to God. And even though we are at different churches today, and have been for the last seven years, his influence in my life has not faded. We continue to meet once a month, and what began as a friendship in that tiny little church has never ended. I pray it never will.

Along with joining a small group, finding an accountability partner—someone who knows you, who really knows you—is probably the most important and critical part of whatever spiritual growth I have experienced. The willingness to speak honestly and openly with each other cannot be underestimated. Just the realization that each month Dave is going to ask me how I'm doing in areas of faith, family, and personal struggles forces me to remain strong and helps me in moments of weakness.

Thanks, Dave, for being willing to invest your time in my life.

A CHANGED LIFE

I met men like these and others who would influence my walk with God in this very small church. One man who has had a tremendous place in my life is Alan Gerwig. Like Dave, Alan accepted me for who I was and allowed me to be myself. Fortunately, Alan is still my friend and continues to be a positive influence in my life, even though as with Dave, we attend different churches today.

I have to say, with a true sense of disbelief, that this man—the same one who was living a life of self-indulgence and self-gratification—has been privileged to preach God's Word as both a pastor and guest speaker on many occasions. All the while, I've been utterly amazed at what God has done and continues to do in me. The changes that have occurred in my life have been monumental. Anyone who has known me for more than fifteen years can attest to that. Bonnie surely can, and not unlike the Lord, she loves me anyway.

About eleven years ago, a guy I was in the navy with called me. It just so happened to be my fortieth birthday. I was just about to go out with Bonnie and my son, John, for Chinese food. when the phone rang. When I said hello, I heard this voice from the past say," Johnny? This is Mikey." Mikey was Mike Interbartolo, from the North End of Boston. This was a guy I hung out with a lot. Several of us used to hang out a lot and party together even more.

The reason for telling you this is that as we talked and reminisced a bit, he said he had been thinking about coming to Florida. I don't know how many of you can relate to this, but at first, I was kind of put back. After a hesitation that probably lasted longer than it should, I said, "That would be cool." His response was that we could get together and party. It was then I told him, "I don't really party anymore." I went on to say that I was a Christian now.

He asked, "A Christian? Well, how big a Christian are you?"

My answer, which still makes me smile, was, "Pretty big!" After a few more minutes of small talk, I said good-bye. Mikey never did come down and has not called back. I sincerely hope it was not because of anything I said. But I am glad I got to tell him about the change the Lord has made in my life. My prayer is that he is making those same kinds of changes in his.

As I look back on the period of time I spent indulging in the excesses of life, I can honestly say I do not regret them. You may be shocked or even appalled to read that, but I believe everything I am and have and will become is related to the trials and tribulations that I went through. I am sure it was not God's plan that I went through them. I am sure He would have rather I trust Him and rely on Him sooner than I did. But I know that He used that period and those struggles to refine me and to mold me into what He wants me to be I am certain of that, and I am certain He continues to do that in my life. One thing is for sure: there are a lot of rough edges and a lot of work still to be done. I am just so grateful He does not grow weary.

Most of the things I was involved in and the things I have gone through could have been avoided, and most of them should have been avoided. But the Lord has allowed me to be able to relate to an entirely different group of people because of these experiences. I don't believe this is in spite of those experiences, I believe it is a direct result of those experiences. I am glad I survived long enough to see Him in the midst of it all.

The Lord continues to amaze me by allowing me to be used by and for Him. This is coming from a man who spent so many years trying to escape his reality and one who can honestly say unequivocally to anyone who would ask that today, I am determined to embrace it. If someone like me can be used by God, He truly can and will use anyone.

My hope and prayer is that I will always be willing to answer Him when He calls. One thing I have learned is that in order to be able to hear Him when He calls, I have to learn to listen for Him. As I am sure you can identify with and as Elijah reminds us, He doesn't always speak to us by way of a storm or out of an earthquake. Sometimes, "He speaks to us in a still small voice."

There is a question I have considered over the years. It is a simple one but, in many ways, a profound one. The question is, what is the evidence of Christ in a person? I believe the answer is equally as simple. It is a "changed life". If we can agree this is true, I am a living example of what the Lord can do. Yes, the Lord can even change someone like me.

If you are reading this and you know anything about me at all, you know this is true. The Lord has changed me from the inside out. He has kneaded this chunk of clay and continues to do so today. My prayer is that He never stops.

Thank you, Jesus, for loving me! I am not a theologian or a Biblical scholar and do not profess or pretend to be one. I am simply a man who loves Jesus and wants to be used by Him for His glory. I hope with all my heart that this will be considered as you read further.

The World is watching

Keeping the World Out
(We Must Protect God?)

M y experiences during these last twelve or so years have prompted me to communicate what I have seen in a way that does not cast judgment (one of the primary problems I will talk about), yet still allows me to share with you what I have seen during that time. As I said earlier, it is my sincere hope to be constructive, not critical. I guess that, too, will be subject to the perceptions or presuppositions you may or may not have as you give thought to my assertions and reflections.

Not unlike most who have found themselves serving in a church's inner circle, I have been witness to many things that have been said and done in the name of the Lord by people who, in most cases, genuinely believe they are doing God's will. But for me, there is one thing that stands above the rest. It is what I feel is a deep-rooted belief that we must not allow the "world" to enter the Church. In many cases, it is this belief that has caused the current worldview of the Church in America, a worldview that perceives the "Church of Jesus Christ" as one filled with hypocrisy, judgment, and a sense of superiority. This view that, in many cases, is well deserved and sadly, undeniable in many more cases.

Ravi Zacharias said in his book and video series, <u>Deliver Us from Evil</u>, copyright 1996, Word publishing, in the 1950's and 1960's, the church closed its doors to the world, and in so doing, lost their social significance. Can this be true? Could the most powerful movement of God in the history of mankind have lost their social significance in America? Worse yet, if this is true, is the Church aware of this, or perhaps more important, does it even matter to those of us who claim to be the Church?

I know we are all familiar with the question, what would Jesus do? My question regarding this last statement is a simple one. What would Jesus *say*? Is this the Church He left behind, the one He charged with carrying on His work and with feeding and loving His sheep?

The effort the Church has made to distinguish itself from the world has not been seen by the world as the presence of Jesus Christ. Quite the contrary; it has been seen by the world as an ugliness that has no place in the Church. It has been seen by the world as the Church separating itself from the world, and quite frankly, this effort to do so has had the opposite effect from what Jesus' statement in Acts 1:8 implies, we were to have had on the world.

His Words in this passage were to encourage us and to let us know He would empower us through His Holy Spirit, as we consider the opportunity we have to be His witnesses. Somehow, it seems for many this is no longer an opportunity or privilege, somewhere along the way, it has become our right and is only shown to those we deem worthy.

Unfortunately, instead of the Church being seen by the world as a witness to or for Jesus Christ, and in many cases because of the Church's fear of tarnishing its own image in a self-absorbed delusion of superiority, the world has been witness to a Church that has brought disdain and mistrust among those Jesus came to save—the Lost—of which we, who call on His name as Savior, were once a part.

God did not call us or equip us to "make disciples" in a world that looks like us, acts like us, and is in agreement with us. Did He? He has called us and equipped us to go into the world, into this world. This dark, dirty, lost world is in need of the same Savior we each needed and still do. This can be accomplished without being of the world. However, I want to exclaim that this cannot be accomplished without being in the world! This bears repeating. This cannot be accomplished without us being in the world!

So here lies the problem for many. How can we do this? How can we be in this world and yet not be of it? The answer is simple. We do it the same way Jesus did: by placing our faith and trust in God, by going where He sends us, by doing what He has asked us to do, and by living lives that point others to Him. It cannot be accomplished by lives that are pointing at them. The world needs us to be *in* it. If we are not, how will they know? How did we lose sight of the need to be in the world? How did we become isolated from the world? These are the questions we must answer if we are going to determine where God is in His Church. Surely, we must want to know.

Are we afraid? If so, we must remember He has given us the protection we need to be in the world by giving us, His Holy Spirit, His Word, and the "Full armor of God" as described in Ephesians 6 HCSB. He needs and wants us to follow Him and to reach out to the Lost. If this were not so, would He have left us to spread His Gospel?

He needs us to serve Him by sharing Him with those we come in contact with, those who are lost, those who are searching, and those who are in need of a Savior. He does not need us to protect Him! Do you hear me? Let me reiterate: He does not need us to protect Him!

Jesus wants us to place our trust, our reliance, and our faith in Him and then to go boldly into this world and make disciples.

This seems to be something many in the Church today have forgotten. God the Father (the Creator), Jesus Christ (the Son, the Savior of mankind), and the Holy Spirit (the Counselor), who now lives in each of us who knows Him, is a *Missionary God* and is still in the business of carrying out His Mission: saving those who are lost. I praise Him every day for not having seen me as unworthy or too far gone for Him to reach me and shame on me, or us, if we see this world as somehow unworthy of this same grace and perhaps equally as sad, as unfit for a place in His church.

In essence, this is what led me to title this book, *Where Is God in His Church?* It is this notion that we must separate ourselves from the world and cannot allow the world to infiltrate the Church that has led me to ask this question. As I have said, I believe this question comes as a direct result of a fear many in the Church have today: the fear that if we are not careful, the Church may begin to look like the world. I contend this fear is unwarranted, because the Church began to look like the world the moment you and I arrived.

That is a sobering thought, isn't it? I hope so. It is intended to be, because I think we need to be completely sober and very much aware of the perception the world has of us, the Church. Sadly, as I said previously, this is a perception that is sometimes well deserved and often justified.

WHERE IS GOD IN HIS CHURCH?

For me, this is a serious question and one that deserves and demands serious consideration. For far too long, we as believers have spent our Sunday mornings attending church and going home unchanged. Many of us, it would appear, have no real concern with the effect that our lives have on the Lost in regard to our faith or in our witness for Jesus.

Unfortunately, some have become convinced they need to behave a certain way, look a certain way, and even talk a certain way in order to give the appearance of righteousness. The idea, I suppose, is to present a sort of Christ-likeness to the world. But if we look at the life of our Lord, this is not the example we see, is it? Wasn't He the same all the time, and weren't others drawn to Him? Didn't He look like them, talk like them, and live with them? If so, doesn't that mean He was in the world? By doing so, wasn't He able to influence them, empower them, equip them, and then, ultimately, send them out to represent Him? Are we not the continuation of that plan?

Where did we go wrong? What has caused us to lose focus on His plan for His Church? Certainly, many factors have contributed to this reality, but perhaps one of the most damaging ones for the Church has been the lack of consistency. Consistency is critical to our faith and how we are viewed by our world. Jesus was a great example of such a lifestyle. Even in the face of His own death, He still lived as an example of grace and mercy for those who would choose to crucify Him.

It is this lack of consistency that perpetuates the world's impression of the Church. In the eyes of those outside the Church, we judge them for how they live, and statistics prove we live the same way. We take political positions and espouse points of view that are seen by the world as authoritative, all the while professing to be submissive to God.

Maybe you can say this is not true for you and your church or fellowship. But for many in the Church today, Sunday mornings have become a time when they are completely different people than they are the rest of the week. I ask myself constantly, *Am I the same at work, at home and at play as I am at church?* I hope so. What about you? We look a little more into this need to be consistent later.

So, where is God in His Church?

To some, this may seem like a silly question. You may have a quick answer, like He is in the hearts of those who know Him. Or He is omnipresent, so He is everywhere. I have no real argument for or against either of these comments.

However, I am searching for a more specific answer to this question, and it is based on the awareness that where He is in our churches may not be evident to everyone, especially to those who don't know Him.

Do you think this is a possibility in your church or fellowship? Could someone come there on any given Sunday and leave believing he has encountered God? Or do you suppose one could leave unaware of where God was? I think this is a very real question and should be a very real concern for His Church. So I ask you again, where is God in His Church?

The answer, and my contention, is that He is where we have placed Him.

If we have created an altar we believe He occupies, is that not where He is to us? Or maybe He is in the sanctuary. If we have built a building that on each Sunday morning we refer to as the "House of the Lord," is that not where He is? Once again, where is God in His Church? He is where we have placed Him.

If He is at the center of our churches, it will be evident, and our world and community will know. We will know. If He is hidden away behind a religion that has long since lost its appeal and is in a constant state of decline, that will be evident, too. We will know that as well.

If He is at the center of our personal lives, it will also be evident, and those in our world and in our neighborhoods will know. The people we work with will know, and the people we hang out with will know. So what about you and me? Where have we placed Him? Where has the Church placed Him? Is this question disconcerting to you? I hope so, because it should be.

These questions are very revealing if we ask them of ourselves. If not, we will just simply continue to hold onto our religion, even at the cost of our relationships with Him and with the Lost He came to save. Do you hear me? Could that be the case in your life or in your church? Has it become more important to maintain the religion you grew up with than to reach the Lost who live next door? If this is the case, is the world wrong in its perception of the Church?

As I write this and you read it, I am sure there are some who have already concluded there is some sort of bias that causes me to think of the Church in this way. To many, asking such questions about God's bride may point to some sort of blasphemy or even a specific problem they believe exists in today's Church.

They may conclude this is one of the major problems with the Church today, proclaiming that in their day, no one would have ever asked such a question. They may communicate that they were content to just believe that God is with us.

Perhaps there are others who disagree, even to the point of discrediting my contentions all together. If you find yourself in this camp, I challenge you to read further.

The challenge is simply to read on and allow the Lord to open the eyes of your heart to the possibility that everything is not as it should be in the Church, in your church, and in your life.

The truth is there is such a view, and even though you may not share it or even agree with it, it is no less real for some. It exists in our world today and has validity to those who uphold it. If we take the time to consider what others say, maybe we can help them see it differently. If not, how can we make a difference in their worldview at all?

Do you hear what I am telling you?

We, the Church, need to consider everyone's view of us and of His Church if we are to ever be able to show them the light of Christ. If we are to be able to help them see things from a different viewpoint, it has to start by realizing they have one.

I want to assure anyone who may take the time to read this that it is not my intention to disparage the Church. I am only trying to point out the reality that exists among those around us who do not belong to a fellowship (church) and, because of what they perceive and their presuppositions, do not intend to join one. This is something I think we have to do if we are going to reach the Lost. If we don't do it, they may never find Jesus.

I know the Lord left instructions on how we are to live our lives and what we are to do regarding reaching the Lost. My question is simply, am I doing it? Are you doing it? Are we living our lives the way He intended? If we can say we are or that we are trying to, my next question is, why doesn't the world around us see us the way we see ourselves? Why do they see so many things so differently than we do? Are we simply out of touch? Have we been huddled for so long that we have forgotten our purpose or, perhaps, His purpose for us as His followers? You may want to say the enemy has blinded them. This is certainly a very real possibility. But they may also be unwilling to participate because of what they see in us. I would like us to consider the possibility we are not reflecting Jesus very well.

Countless books have been written that deal with problems in the Church, and they are fine in their own right. Scholars, which I have already confessed I am not, are constantly writing book after book to help the Church and its people find their way through an ever-changing world.

Many churches never experience change, even though they may spend all of their time equipping or preparing one another to deal with this ever-changing world. Does this sound familiar? Are you in a church like that? Is your church still the same as it was decades ago? If so, do you realize the world all around you has changed and you have not? It is God's Word that never changes, not His Church. It has to change to reach the community that surrounds it.

As I have said, for every question I am asking, there is likely a book that has been written by someone of much greater intelligence than I.

It is being read by people with equal or greater intelligence. Yet, the problems that continue to exist go unchanged and, in a lot of cases, grow worse every day.

The world is changing and continuing to grow further and further away from God and His Church. Ironically, many in the Church just continue to do the same things that they have always done. They are not applying what they have learned to their lives and, quite honestly, have no intention of ever doing so.

Perception Is Reality

One such book for me, which is one of the best resources I have found that deals directly with these premises about the Church in America, is a book by David Kinnaman of the Barna group called, *The UnChristian*.

If you are not familiar with the Barna Group, they are statisticians, and their findings are the result of countless hours of studies and research and are very difficult to dispute. *The UnChristian* speaks directly about the current state of the Church in America and the way it is seen by not only by those in our communities and our world but also by those within the Church itself. For me, this is where the idea that *perception is reality* is communicated in a very clear and concise way.

Unfortunately, the findings regarding this perception for those who have come in contact with the Church of Jesus Christ, as we have touched on, is not always a pretty sight. Almost equally as disconcerting in my experience is that the defense of the Church among believers regarding this statement has become so unwavering that many I have talked to have argued this statement in itself is untrue

How can anyone say this? If we are perceived by a lost and dying world as hypocritical, judgmental, and with a sense of superiority, how can we look at them and dispute their perception of reality? If we are disputing their perceptions, doesn't it give evidence to their claims and ultimately give justification to their point of view? When we do so, are we not giving credence to their point of view? We have to start by acknowledging that everyone's perception is their reality: yours, mine, and theirs.

You and I may not like it, but this fact cannot be debated and certainly cannot be dismissed. If you disagree with my assertion, ask yourself a simple question. If you perceive something to be a certain way, is that not how it is for you? What can be done to change your perception? It can only be changed if you perceive something differently.

What can we do then? What must we do?

What we can do is try to help people change their perceptions by showing them a different reality. How do we do this? I believe we start by accepting their right to have their viewpoint by realizing it is based on their perception of reality.

What we do not need to do is try to persuade them their reality is wrong. This would give certainty to the perspective they have been espousing all along.

So, what can we do? What do we need to do? We need to start by introducing them to a new reality. How can we do this?

We can start the same way Jesus did: by looking at them, listening to them, and loving them. We can start by showing them Christ-like love. This kind of love is disarming, isn't it?

Don't you think we have to get people to lay down their defenses if we are going to be able to show them who Jesus is to us? Nothing breaks through barriers quite like love. If we do not have love, we are a, "sounding gong or a clanging cymbal ." 1 Corinthians 13:1 HCSB

If you didn't grow up in the Church, as I didn't, you can probably remember the people and places you went to that gave stock to your perceptions or presuppositions or dispelled them. In my case, each person or place that dispelled them did so by showing me grace and Christ-like love. They didn't have to do this for me; they chose to, and it is because of their willingness to treat me in this way that my resistance was overcome. I became open not only to the messenger but, ultimately, to the Message. For me, it was their love for me that pointed to their love for Him and, ultimately, to my desire to know that love.

I'll never forget the time when I was about twenty years old and had long hair. As I told you, I had started attending church because of my soon-to-be wife, and they had meet-and-greet time every Sunday. I kid you not: there were people who avoided shaking my hand. I can only say that my perception was that they did it because of my appearance. The reason I believe this was true was, shortly after cutting my hair, many of the same people shook my hand without hesitation. Was my perception wrong? Perhaps, but it was then and still is my perception. They did nothing to change it, and quite honestly, I never wanted them to.

I am telling you this to reinforce the notion that our perceptions are very real to us, and sometimes, as with mine, they have lasting implications in our lives.

Our example is Jesus. Jesus did not use His deity as a means to dissuade others from the views that they held. He simply used His ability to see into and to speak to their hearts as a means of sharing His love with them.

Shouldn't those of us who call ourselves Christ followers do the same? Shouldn't we follow His example? Is it more important to show love to someone or to have him believe he is wrong in the way he views us? I hope the answer is obvious.

So, when someone says the Church is hypocritical, judgmental, and has a sense of superiority, we do not need to try and discredit him or to defend the Church. What we need to do is to try and help him see it differently.

Once again, it is not our place, nor should it be an effort on our part, to protect God or the Church. It should be our place to represent Him well to the world by our reactions to their contentions.

I think it also important to interject here that it is not our place to judge the Lost or others according to Paul in Romans 2:1 HCSB. It is necessary for us to understand that we, the Church, are being judged by the world and in far too many cases, we have been found wanting.

Wouldn't Christ be better served if we were to address their views rather than deny them? How does defending against their view of the Church demonstrate the love of Jesus to a lost and dying world? How can you defend something about yourself that someone else sees in you? If you tell me I am rude, and my response to you is, "No I am not." Does that make your view of me any different? Obviously not. In fact, it just gives credence to your contention, doesn't it?

Did Paul not say in Romans 12:20 HCSB, "If your enemy is thirsty give him something to drink, if he is hungry, give him something to eat. In doing this you will be heaping burning coals on his head." Doesn't this mean we are to let our lives demonstrate our faith, so no fault can be found with us? Should we see those with this perception of us or the Church as enemies of the Church? And if we say yes, how should we respond to them? Remember, our response may very well give credence to their claims—or not. So, when we take on the responsibilities associated with being the defender of the Church, we also take on the responsibility of representing it by our words and deeds.

I don't know about you, but for me, this can be a daunting thing to consider.

Remember what 1 Peter 3:15, tells us: "But in your hearts set apart Christ as Lord. Always be prepared to give an answer to everyone who asks you to give the reason for the hope that you have. But do this with gentleness and respect." Is this how we respond to a world if we are defending our faith? Is this how we respond to a world that sees us differently than we see ourselves? Would their stated perceptions of hypocrisy, judgment, and sense of superiority point to a defense of the Gospel, like Peter describes?

Please do not misunderstand me here. My intention is not to suggest we have to compromise our beliefs. Quite the contrary. I am suggesting we live what we believe before the world and then we can let our lives, which will reflect Jesus and our faith in Him, be what they see. Can we truly deny that the Church doesn't reflect the perception many have of it?

I can almost hear the argument for maintaining the sanctity of the Church in a lot of cases with the belief of the necessity of keeping God's house pure and reverent. My contention would be we lost that opportunity the moment that you and I arrived. I am sorry if that is offensive to anyone, but none of us were any different in our state before we accepted Jesus than those who have not yet accepted Him.

The fundamental issue for the Church is spelled out in Jesus' last words in the passages in Matthew 28:16–20, where He commands us to, "Go and tell others about the Good News," and in Acts 1:8, where He tells us, "the Holy Spirit will come upon us and we will be His witnesses." Is that we, the Church are responsible for the Jesus that the Lost of our world sees. We have been commissioned and empowered by Him through the Holy Spirit to share Him and show Him to those we come in contact with.

Is that what the world sees when it looks at the Church? Is that what the Church is to them?

Let me repeat that this way: what the world sees when it looks at the Church is what the Church is to them. Even more dramatically is the reality that what the world sees when it looks at the Church is how Jesus looks to them, and when the world looks at us, we are how they see Him.

We need to ask ourselves a simple question. What is it they are seeing? The answer is they are seeing exactly what we are showing them. The next question really needs to be is that what we want them to see? Can you answer yes to that question? I have to admit I don't always want others to think of Jesus based on what they see in me.

Certainly, the Church has been seen to be involved in numerous humanitarian efforts throughout its history. When and where there is a crisis or disaster, the Church is usually the first to pitch in and lend a hand. The Church has responded, and there is no doubt the world is watching.

Unfortunately, we live in a, "What have you done for me lately," world, and the enemy exploits and magnifies every slipup of the Church. I tell people in my company or in churches that I have been a part of and served in, "One 'ah shoot' wipes out a thousand 'at-a-boys.'" The Church is involved in a lot of big picture ways that definitely are its responsibility and part of its Mission. But it is the small things that take away from the perception of good. It's the small things that tend to have the biggest effect, because they are more easily seen and more often demonstrated.

Wouldn't it be great if the world saw us as Jesus intends—as the Body of Christ?

Judgment—
The Sins of the World

The Church today seems very quick to point out the sins of the world. The premise appears to be if the world would only turn from their sins and be like us, everything would be better. The continuing rhetoric that is given by many in the Church today is that if the world would follow our example like they used to that the world would be a better place.

Pardon me here, but how misguided can we be?

Every time the Church speaks out against a particular sin, it stands in judgment (again, Rom. 2:1) of that sin, and it better make sure it is without any sin itself, especially the one it is speaking out against. Every time the Church cries foul or calls out others for anti-Christian bias, it better be sure it is not demonstrating bias toward another group or against the world.

Can we say that? Is the Church in America unbiased?

Let me rephrase that: would those outside the Church in America see it as unbiased? Would those outside the church you attend see it as unbiased? I think we do not have to look very far to know the answer to that question is a resounding no.

Again and again, our culture, media, and government can be seen casting stones at the Church. You might ask, but didn't Jesus tell us we would be persecuted and put to death, and hated by all nations because of Him (Matthew 24:9 HCSB)? The answer is obviously yes. But, what about when He told us to, "turn the other cheek (Matthew 5:39 HCSB), to judge not or we would be judged by the same measure (Matthew 7:2 HSCB)"? Doesn't that apply here?

You see, Einstein's theory of relativity really is true. For every action, there really is an equal and opposite reaction. It is no different for the Church. Everything we do and everything we say has an effect. Doesn't it?

The question is what kind of effect are we having? Once again, if we can find common ground in our understanding that the world's view of the Church is not always a good one, we can be united in our hope to see that view change.

We have to be aware of the reality that the way we behave can either add to someone's view or dispel it. We may not think about it or even want to consider it, but we do have an effect.

So, if we can say that this is true. Shouldn't it be high on our list of priorities to want them to see us, the Church, or even more important, Jesus in a different light? I would like you to stop here for just a moment, and ask yourself if you agree that your life is having an effect on how someone you know and care about views Jesus. I don't know about you, but for me, this is very humbling and often causes me to ask forgiveness.

One of my greatest fears has always been that the way someone perceives me or my faith in Christ may cause him or her to have a view that may take away from Jesus and His Mission. Because of me or my witness, that perception may very well cause the individual to miss out on an opportunity to know Him.

Can we really afford to have that kind of a reaction? I pray all of us can agree that we cannot.

You and I can argue that the perceptions and the bias the world has of the Church are wrong. Or you may say that all they need to do is to spend time in the Church, and they would see their perceptions are not true. The problem with this argument is that many have already made up their minds, and for most, it is based on their own experiences or the experiences of someone they know. For many, it is because they have spent time in the Church that they have developed these views or perceptions. It is because of what they have experienced.

The views expressed by many are earned by the Church. The statistics and the reality of declining membership and failing churches give credence to these claims. The sad reality is that in many cases within the Church, it doesn't seem to be a major concern—or at least not enough of one to see the need to address these perceptions. Maintaining the status quo or keeping Church the way we believe it should be has, for many, become the most important aspect of their church experience. The real question for us as believers should be are we more concerned with maintaining our vision of the Church, or are we more concerned with helping others find Jesus and their place in His Church?

Is it about our vision, or is it about His Mission?

As with most of the questions I pose, only you and I can answer them as they relate to our specific situations. As with the people I reference (the world around us), we also have our own perceptions, which are our realities as we consider our churches or fellowships.

We know where our heart is and what it is we need to do to help people overcome their perceptions. Whether we deem them to be right, wrong, or indifferent isn't—or shouldn't be—the issue. The issue is they have these perceptions, and that makes them real to them.

The pivotal question is, does it matter to us? Are we willing to do what is necessary to help change these perceptions, even if you struggle with whether they are real or justified? Or do we believe the Church is here for us to meet our needs, to be the way we like it: the way it has always been for many since they were children? I am not sure about you, but I know Jesus was clear in His message to us to carry the Gospel forward, and to reach all people in all places, crossing all cultural barriers. In acknowledging that, we have to acknowledge the Church must be aware of the way it may be being perceived by the world and be willing to see its need to change, and to make those changes as the world around it changes. If not, what is the point?

Change Is Inevitable

All this talk of perceptions and viewpoints, of how we're seen or not seen, of who sees us this way and why, brings us to the most controversial thing in the churches I have been involved with over the last twelve years: change!

Change, if we are honest and really think about it, is probably the most difficult thing we do as people. And it is no different for the Church. However, the one thing I have to point out—and with which you cannot disagree—is change is inevitable. Change happens every day. If you have children, you can see it when they are born and as you watch them grow up. You can see it when you look in the mirror or when you look at your parents or your spouse. Can't you? If you can admit that this is true, how can anyone believe it doesn't or shouldn't take place in the Church?

Is the Church immune to change? If so, how does it reach the next generation, ethnic group, or culture with the Gospel? My contention here is if it doesn't change, we don't reach them.

An elder at a church where I was an associate and then the interim pastor approached me on a Sunday evening, just before a congregational meeting. He pulled me aside and he told me, "You can stop it now." When I asked him what he was talking about, he said, "You have made your point, and you can stop it now. There are a lot of people here that think that you believe the church has to change."

I answered him, "I do believe that the church does have to change."

His response astounded me. He answered in a very matter-of-fact way, "I don't think so. There is nothing wrong with maintaining a sense of tradition and reverence in the sanctuary."

Was he wrong? I guess in theory no, not necessarily, but how does, "tradition and reverence in the sanctuary," correspond to a culture that doesn't know much about the Church, and what they do know, they don't like.

Can this maintenance of the, "tradition and reverence in the sanctuary," help bring people closer to Jesus? Please understand, I am not asking you if it brings you closer to Him. I am asking you if it brings the Lost closer to Him. There is a difference, don't you think?

If the world doesn't know who Jesus is, can it really understand the need for tradition and reverence in a building? Furthermore, is it more important to maintain this, "tradition and reverence," than to reach into our communities so that they can understand who Jesus is and how they can come to know Him? Forgive me, but if we can't see the flaw in this type of thinking, that is precisely where the problem lies. The problem is that if this is the way that the Church is seen by the world than this is the way the Church is to the world .

There is a song from the sixties by a rock-and-roll group called the Byrds. "Turn, Turn, Turn" is the title of the song, and it speaks about the third chapter of the book of Ecclesiastes. This song, as with the book, speaks directly about the reality of change in our lives. Interestingly, because of this song, Solomon's words have been embraced by a secular world, as this song points to the reality of constant change, of a time or a season for everything under heaven.

In verses 1 through 8 of Ecclesiastes, Solomon points this out by saying, "There is a season for everything in our lives," and that all these seasons, periods, or moments in time have been made by God to occur in His time for each of us.

Is this true? Can we see evidence of this in our own lives? Can you see evidence of it in your life? We don't have to look far, do we?

It can be seen in our situations, in our circumstances, and in our lives all the time. We can see it easily in recent times because of economic situations that have brought changes to many of our lives. Some of us may have experienced the loss of a loved one or the birth of a child.

We can easily see the seasons of our lives and the changes that occur by looking in the mirror or at pictures of the times that have passed. Our memories are constant reminders of the changes in our lives that have unfolded over time. Our lives are progressing through these seasons as we live them, aren't they? We can clearly see the changes as they occur in all the phases of our lives.

Perhaps the easiest place to see changes is in our physical life. Our lives begin at conception. From there, we begin to grow into a person. During the next nine months, we develop, grow, and become a baby. We grow into children, to adolescents, and to adults.

But the change doesn't stop there, does it?

If we look in the mirror as life goes by, we can see the continued change that takes place in our bodies. We go from a young adult, with strength and stamina, to the peak of our physical strength and abilities. From there, we begin to see the decline of our physical bodies. We start to see our hair change color or fall out altogether. For men at least, we start to see that maybe the Lord does have a sense of humor, as we begin to notice hair growing in what would appear to be unnecessary places. Perhaps we have pain we never before noticed. We begin to be, as my friend Dave told me one time, "the used to guy"—"I used to do this," or, "I used to do that." Ultimately, our physical bodies will fail us, and we will die, unless the Lord should return beforehand.

Change doesn't only take place in our physical bodies, does it?

Change takes place in the intellectual areas of our lives as well. As with our physical bodies, when we are born, we are completely helpless and totally dependent on our parents.

Eventually, we learn to talk, first with one word and then with several until we can form sentences. We are then given the opportunity to learn to read, write, and solve problems.

Each of us reaches our intellectual potential at different points in our lives, but we do have a peak of our intellectual skills and abilities. In time, we begin to have more difficulty focusing, or perhaps we just can't remember like we used to. For some, it is just a nuisance; for others, it becomes debilitating.

The changes that occur in our intellectual abilities, as with our physical bodies, are gradual and may go seemingly unnoticed. Our physical and intellectual natures have limitations, and we generally give in to those limitations out of necessity, if for no other reason. Try though we might over time and by necessity, we ultimately surrender ourselves to this reality.

We have changed!

The other area I want us to consider when we think about the inevitability of change is our Spiritual lives. In Ecclesiastes 3:11 HCSB, Solomon says, "God has placed eternity in the hearts of men." Therefore, we understand that we do have a built-in desire to know Him or seek to know Him, and when we come to the place where we accept Jesus as our Lord and Savior, our Spiritual journey begins. We become a new creation. This happens at different times in our lives for each of us. Some accept Him as a child and some later in life. And by the grace of God, many do so at the end of their physical lives.

Paul reminds us of this in 2 Corinthians 5:17 HCSB: "Therefore if anyone is in Christ, there is a new creation; old things have passed away, and look, new things have come. When we accept Him at whatever point, we are made new, we are set apart, we are sanctified by Christ"

We are forever changed, Praise God!

It is because of this that we begin to view the world through a different lens. Our hearts and our minds begin to be drawn to the things of God, and we begin to grow. We start to feel convicted when we are involved in areas of our lives that are not conducive of God and His plan for us. We become aware, or at least more aware, of our need to be people of prayer and students of God's Word.

And in direct contrast to our mental and or physical selves, we continue to grow in our faith and knowledge of God until He returns or we are called Home to be with Him in paradise. Our Spiritual lives do not die. Though we may certainly experience valleys, we also experience mountaintops. But unlike our physical and mental lives, our spiritual life does not fail us over time.

What about you? Does this sound like your spiritual experience? Do you view the world through the lens of grace? Are you a person of prayer? Are you a student of God's Word? Are you still growing in your relationship to Him? Is your experience progressive? Have you changed from how you were before you accepted Jesus? Are you still changing and growing in your knowledge and love for the Lord?

What do these three aspects of our lives have in common? First, they are all created by God. Second, they all have a beginning, and they are all progressive. Finally, it is God's plan for us to enjoy each of them.

What else do they have in common? They are all in a constant state of change! The physical and intellectual areas of our lives reach a certain level and, through time, erode and ultimately die. But our Spiritual lives live on forever, continuing to grow and change.

Do you agree with these assertions? If so, how can there be any argument that the Church does have to change? Simply because everything changes, doesn't it? Please don't misunderstand me here: God's Word never changes, His promises never change, but His Church—His Missional Church—has to change in order to reach the next generation with His timeless message.

Simply put, life is progressive. Each day is a new beginning. Our time is appointed and *change is inevitable*. We can choose to embrace this truth, or we can run from it. But we cannot escape it.

There is an occasion for everything and a time for every activity under heaven. Ecclessiastes 3:1 HCSB

If our mission is to bring the Church of Jesus Christ to the world, we have to accept that their perceptions and viewpoints are their own and very real to them, and we are going to have to care enough to see the need to help change those perceptions!

Relevant or Irrelevant

Knowing these things and understanding the reality of change in our lives should help us to understand that change itself is not only necessary but inevitable, unavoidable, and not something to be feared. None of this will matter to us unless we admit the need for change. This can and will happen only if we see change as worthwhile.

Interestingly enough to me is the same ideas that keep others from seeing the Church the way we see it can keep us from seeing it the way they do. We must remember that our enemy never sleeps and is victorious when the Church is deemed useless or out of touch by the Lost Jesus came and died to save.

As we move forward, I hope we can clearly see change is a part of God's plan for each of us. It is change that will lead the Church to be always relevant to the world and has given it a prominent place in the world.

Oh no, I said it, the word that drives traditionalists crazy and makes contemporary churches feel justified in whatever they do.

Relevant!

This is a word that has become both divisive and destructive in far too many cases. It is something that seems to rock the very foundation of the Church. Is that possible? If the Church is built on the "Rock of Jesus Christ," can anything rock its foundation?

Is maintaining the traditions of the past the foundation on which we have built our churches? Then yes, they can, and they should, definitely and quite frankly, be rocked. But if it is the timeless truth of Jesus and His Word on which we build our churches, nothing can or will rock them. Maybe we need to ask ourselves on what foundation we have built our churches. On what foundation have you built the church you attend or serve? When is the last time significant change took place in your church? I don't mean a change of pastor. I mean a change in the culture of your church. Can you answer without wincing or feeling defensive? If not, you have your answer.

As we think about the question of relevance and contemplate what it means to be relevant, I would like us to consider what is relevant to you and me in our everyday lives. Then, we should ask ourselves a simple question: If I don't think something is relevant to me and to my life, am I interested in involving myself in that endeavor?

If our answer is no, and most likely it is, how can we expect people who do not know Jesus or anything about His Church, other than what they may have seen or heard about it—which we have already discussed as being filled with, "hypocrisy, judgment, and a sense of superiority"—to want to be a part of it?

If the Church is deemed to be irrelevant by someone, I think it is safe to say it has no influence in that person's life. And, therefore, the individual has no interest in being a part of it.

Is this the Church of Jesus Christ? Then, how and why is it being seen this way by so many?

I don't know about you, but when I look at the Church from the point of view of being irrelevant, it is easy for me to see the difficulty some people have in becoming part of a church fellowship.

The real question is a simple one: are we relevant or irrelevant? Do we matter to our communities and our culture? It is almost insulting, isn't it? If you are a believer and have been for any length of time, isn't it almost a natural reflex to want to defend God and His Word when this question is asked? The only problem is it is not God we end up defending. It is our churches and our fellowships, which, for all intents and purposes, may not be representing God very well, if at all.

Do you feel defensive right now? Have I created a point of contention you would rather avoid? If so, my challenge to you—as to myself—is to consider for a moment that everything I have said is true in the eyes of the world around us. Then, I have to ask, what is our role in changing their perceptions? What is our role in helping the church become relevant to our community? Furthermore, does it matter to us that these perceptions exist? I know I'm repeating the same line of thought here, but I am doing so because it bears repeating. Where is God in His Church? Once again, He is where we have placed Him. If He is leading and the head of our churches, I guarantee we are relevant, and the Lost are coming to know Him.

This is one truth that never changes!

So, are we relevant? One way to find out is simply to consider what the effect would be if we were to close our church or fellowship. Have you ever thought of that? Are you willing to consider it here and now? Would it make a difference? If your church closed, would anyone know you were gone? Does your church or fellowship matter to your community? Not to you or your congregation, but to your community?

Sadly, churches close throughout America every day, and no one notices. Sure, those who were hanging onto it as it takes its last breath are affected. But the community around it remains unchanged. Perhaps they are even unaware the church has closed. If so, it is most likely because they never knew it was there in the first place.

So, is your church or fellowship relevant or irrelevant? You know the answer, I am sure. The question is if you accept it and whether it matters.

I have to offer a disclaimer here for the theologians who may be reading this. I am not talking about God's Word when I ask these questions. It does not need my defense.

It is both timeless and as relevant in our everyday lives and in this world today as it was when it was breathed into its writers by the Holy Spirit. I am, however, talking about the Church, and more directly, I am talking to the local church: yours and mine.

If the world deems us irrelevant, how do you suppose they see God's Word? Don't you think that they are one and the same to the world?

Can a group of people or an organization considered irrelevant offer anything to a community they would consider to be relevant? Do we change this perspective by verbally defending or denying it, or do we show them something different? I hope and pray we can all see the need for the latter.

If you have a struggle with hearing the world may see the Church as irrelevant and with giving any credence to what I am saying, I would like to ask you again to consider your own church or, perhaps, even your own life. How would they hold up when viewed through this lens? What would someone's perception be if they watched you or me? If they knew nothing about Jesus and went to your church or spent a week with you on the job, would they hear you share your belief in Jesus? Would they see Jesus reflected in what they heard or saw? Would it be evidenced by your countenance or your attitude toward everyday life and others? Would they sense love, grace, mercy, and forgiveness in your demeanor? Would they deem you or your faith as a relevant part of their lives?

What if we took it a step further. What if they were to come and live with you in your house; would they be blessed by the way you live, or would they be shocked by what others seldom see? Would they be amazed by the way you love your spouse and your children? Or would they be appalled at your behavior? If they were to look into your checkbook, would they see a heart filled with generosity? Or one filled with self-indulgence and overwhelmed by debt?

I can't speak for you, but for me, these are eye-opening things to consider. I am afraid there are many times I would not like the results they would find. Unfortunately, neither would they.

Someone once asked, "If you took everything you had ever said or thought about your neighbors and hung it on a clothesline in your front yard, what would your neighbors think of you?" I don't want to presume to speak for anyone else, but this is a sobering thing for me to consider.

My contention is that the answer to each of those questions is supposed to be yes, and it also needs to be yes when they look at our churches. And when they see our thoughts on the clothesline, they should see the same grace shown to them that Jesus has shown to each of us.

Unfortunately, I have a sneaking suspicion—and I don't even think it is much of a stretch—this is not the case in most of our lives. Most of us, and God himself, might be better served if they don't get to see us up that close.

However, as bad as the former may be to consider, if we can say yes to these questions, if we are willing to have someone view our churches and our lives from the inside, we are living a life and are involved in a church or fellowship that will be both relevant and effective. This is the way Jesus intended it to be. And when we are able to do this, the results will be seen by the world, and those we come in contact with will be attracted to it. This is what caused the Lord to add to their numbers daily those who were saved in that first church in the book of Acts, chapter 2.

Those on the outside of this fellowship, the community and the culture around them, saw genuine faith and love lived out before them. It was different from their world, yet it was in their world and was relevant to their world. They were drawn to it by the power of the Holy Spirit. They were not repelled from it by a sense of unworthiness or inferiority. They didn't see a hint of judgment or hypocrisy. In fact, the results were just the opposite. They were drawn to these people and this fellowship by a sense of belonging, community, and love.

Let me ask one more question. Does my world or your world reflect Jesus like this? It is a simple and direct question that really deserves a simple and direct answer. Can you give it a simple and direct answer? Or would now be a good time to say something like," Well, that is according to your perspective or your point of view."

It is funny how perception can so easily be reality when we look at our own lives. As a church in your community, are you relevant or irrelevant? Ask your neighbor and then ask yourselves.

Keeping Out Outsiders

We have taken a brief look at change and considered relevance versus irrelevance as it relates to our lives and fellowships. In doing so, I hope I have piqued your interest to the possibility that you need to consider where you and the church you attend are with these conditions. From here, we consider some of the things I have seen firsthand from within a church. A church that considers itself loving, caring, and relevant.

One of the biggest complaints heard from visitors coming to a church for the first time is that they don't feel welcome. I am sure you have heard things like, "The people weren't friendly," or, "No one greeted me personally. They were all spending time with each other and acted like they didn't even know I was there."

Some of them are true, some untrue. Some of them are justified, and others not justified. Either way, they are perceptions held by someone based on personal experience. Can we dispute it? I hope you can see by now that we cannot if that is the way they see it. So what can we do about it? We can start by acknowledging these perceptions exist and then do our best to ensure they are not recurring problems.

It has been said that a person decides in the first two minutes whether he is coming back to a church. If this statistic is true, this is before one has heard the music or the message. The church only gets one chance to make a first impression, so it had better be a good one.

Things like the people weren't friendly or I don't fit in are very common and are often not the fault of the church or the people; they are about personal issues or prejudices the individual brought with them when they came. I hope that makes some of you feel better.

I haven't blamed everything relating to the world's perception on the Church. Now I will probably lose the favor that bit of encouragement may give you, as I look at a couple of my personal experiences regarding keeping out outsiders.

My first experience with this type of thinking was at an Elders' meeting. The pastor who had become my best friend told me about a call he received from someone who wanted to use the fellowship hall for a martial arts class. There would be rental fees to the church, and it was an opportunity to give the church some exposure in the community. It would also bring some nonbelievers to our church. Both he and I were in agreement this would be a good thing for everyone involved.

We soon discovered others on the board did not share our view. Quite the contrary. They believed if we did this, we would be opening our church up to Eastern mysticism. I was astonished to the point of being speechless. As for the pastor, I think he was just defeated.

As I would find out later, this group of men had presumed once again to successfully protect God and His Church from the evils of the world, in this case from the evil they perceived in this martial arts class.

We have to begin by asking ourselves if the hearts of the other board members were in the right place? I am certain if you were to ask them, they would say yes, and I am quite sure there are some of you who probably agree with them. But I say a resounding no!

Their hearts were hard and closed to the possibility that God could be at work in their midst. Were they right in their effort not to allow martial arts in the church? I guess that, too, is a matter of perspective. Shouldn't we start with the people and not what they were doing? Is the Church not the place for acceptance and tolerance? Is doing martial arts a sin, or is judging them for doing martial arts a sin?

What were they protecting; or if you share their view, what are you protecting? It must be the congregation, because surely you must know that you are not capable of protecting God. I am sorry if I get a little excited here, but I have a very small window of patience for the idea that the Church is the House of the Lord. The Church is the Body of Christ. The Church is the people, not the building.

As I stated earlier, I am not big on the whole reverence in the sanctuary thinking. In this case, we were presented with an opportunity to allow the world to be involved in the church. Even if it was just by renting the facilities, the chance to allow Lost people to come in contact with those who know Jesus was thwarted. Ironically, those who were lost sought the relationship, and those who know Him stopped it.

Were they right in their assertions? For me, it is obviously no. I think they missed the point completely. We had an opportunity to be an influence for Christ to a group of people and a chance to invite our community into our facility. Prior to this episode, they had already turned away a woman who wanted to rent the facility for a modeling class. I am sure you can probably guess the reason. The girls would be wearing makeup. Keep in mind this was in 1999, not 1899.

Isn't it possible these groups could have been prompted unknowingly by God to ask us for permission to use our facilities and perhaps find Jesus in the process? Do you believe God works like this? I know He does. He prompted me to step outside my comfort zone, and because I did, my life was changed forever. What did we do by saying no to these people? I guess we will not know the answer to that question until the Lord calls us home, and we see Him face to face to give an account of our lives. At the very least, we missed an opportunity to help someone see the Church in a different light than the one they may have seen it in.

In our effort to protect God, we quite possibly continued to fuel the worldview of the Church as judgmental, hypocritical, and having a sense of superiority. This may be conjecture on my part, but the one thing I do know for sure is we managed to keep the world out of this church.

Is the issue here modeling, makeup, martial arts, or Eastern mysticism? No, absolutely not. The issue is whether we are willing and desirous of seeking and accepting the Lost where they are and how they are, the same way you, me, and each of those men were sought after and accepted by Jesus.

It always amazes me how righteous we can become when we are placed in the position of deciding who gets to come. My fear is we don't realize the choice is not ours to make. It is His, and if we don't allow people to come to Him where we are, He will send them to where they will be allowed to come to Him.

The beauty of our Lord is He will not allow those He came to save to be kept out by anyone.

CHRISTIAN YOGA?

When I was serving as an interim pastor, I was overseeing a governing board meeting when one of the board members told me of a lady in the church who was a fitness and yoga instructor. She wanted to make a presentation to the board. Her desire was to serve God with her gift and offer yoga classes at the church to anyone who might be interested.

She came in and made her presentation. You could see right away the sincerity of her heart. It was also very evident that she was a new believer. She seemed very unsure and uncertain of how she would be received. As she began to share, she said she felt this was a way she could serve God; this could be her ministry. She wanted it to be free of charge and to present it as a ministry of the church.

As is my nature, strictly based on her demeanor, my first inclination was to say yes to her request and to proceed with the meeting. But instead, I asked her to put together a program as soon as possible and provide us with an opportunity to pray and consider her request. She should come back to us at our next meeting.

Over the next couple of days, she came back and presented what we had requested. Each person on the board was given a copy of the information, and I asked them to read and pray about it, understanding we would make a decision about it at our next meeting. At that meeting, with very little discussion, the board unanimously approved her request. She was very pleased and excited, and we told her we would put it in the church bulletin on Sunday, and she could place a sign-up sheet in the church foyer.

The next Sunday morning, she did as she was instructed. She had a poster explaining the class, a sign-up sheet, and a black statue about a foot tall of a woman in a yoga position on the table in the foyer. As I came in that Sunday morning, I glanced briefly at her stuff, not thinking much of it, and went on with the service. That evening and into the next week, I received phone calls and letters from people who were appalled to the point of leaving the church because we had allowed another religion into the church.

Their concern was that we were opening the church up to spiritual darkness and that this could not be tolerated. I was amazed by their attitude and still am today. The whole thing was new to me, and I was surprised by the reaction of those involved. I have never seen a group of people so afraid of something that to me seemed so insignificant.

I went on to find out this issue was a huge deal for this very small group of people, and I got to see what can happen when murmuring infects a church. It was leading to genuine division in the church. The intent of a few was to right this wrong, no matter what. They began to mobilize others and to use their influence to promote their position regarding this issue.

There was one couple in particular who immediately began to educate others on the evils of yoga and encourage them to let me and the Elder board know of their concern.

One Friday evening, I was called at home by a lady at the church to come to the women's meeting they were having. The wife of this couple had sat the yoga instructor down and told her of the evils of what she was doing. When my wife and I arrived, the woman was still crying, and we spent the next half an hour or so trying to console her.

After the service the following Sunday, it was communicated to me and to the Elder board by the husband of this particular couple, who happened to be an elder and heading up this group of people, that this was an abomination and had to be stopped, or people were going to leave.

This was a much bigger issue than I had ever imagined, and I had to discover a solution. So, I prayed and came up with something I thought might pacify everyone involved. The solution was very simple, and I believe points to the absurdity of the argument. We would change the name from a yoga class to a stretching and exercise class and remove the statue from the foyer. Amazingly enough, I was able to satisfy the fear of bringing another religion into the church. I say amazingly, because the class was still yoga (we simply changed the name) and the instructor was still the same person, but just by changing the name, we successfully eliminated the threat to our church.

The reason I tell you this story, as with the one concerning martial arts and modeling, is not as I told the man who had seen yoga as evil, to debate the theology surrounding whether these things have a place in the church. It is not to make an issue of their evils, or lack thereof. Rather, I want you to see the effect that was created by the perception these people in this church had, and it was that perception that drove them to their conclusions.

Once what they saw as the problem—in this one case, the word "yoga"—was removed, their perception changed completely. When we changed the name and removed the statue, the perception of what we were doing changed with it. What we were doing did not change!

PERCEPTION IS REALITY.

I truly believe the pretense in each of these cases was to keep the world out of the Church. My question is, for me, a simple one. Do we need to do that? Should we be doing that, and do we have the right to do that? Your answer and your thoughts on these questions are going to be based solely on your point of view, and I respect them. But the harm done to this woman was appalling. The missed opportunity to allow the world to use the church building, even if it was for martial arts and modeling, was missed. And we missed an opportunity to help change someone's view of the Church. Someone may have come to know Jesus through those activities.

One thing I know for sure is in the eyes of those involved, the achieved results were what they had hoped for. The Church was once again safe from the world. Why do you suppose it is the heartfelt desire of so many to keep the world out of the Church? This clearly was not Jesus' plan. He spent all His time with tax collectors and sinners. He ate with them at their houses, He healed their infirmities, and forgave their sins. Does it sound like the men I referred to here would have spent time doing those things? Would they have allowed Jesus to continue meeting and spending time with those kinds of people if He were a part of their church? Sobering to think about in this light, isn't it?

Jesus spent a lot of time speaking directly against the established religious groups and warning them and us of their hypocrisy and wickedness. Unfortunately, as time goes by, we are looking more and more like those people to the world, and if we look in the mirror, it is often easy to see why. Would Jesus see us any differently than those He spoke against in how we have guarded His Church from the world?

If we read the Gospels, it is easy to see Jesus' view on this type of behavior. Somehow, as with those people of His day, we can see it in everyone but ourselves.

The House of the Lord

One Sunday morning, after the incident was resolved and everyone was comfortable with the outcome, I had a man pull me aside to give me perspective on why the statue and/or yoga should not have been allowed in church. His concern was for the Church, because this is the House of the Lord, and we had to be careful what we allowed to be brought into it.

I had known this man for several years, and I always assumed his heart was in the right place. The view he held, this need to keep the Church from being stained by the evils of the world, was genuine and very real to him. This was how he saw the Church. This was his *perception* of reality.

The irony for me was, having known this man for quite some time, I was aware he had a son who was a huge video game fan (as do I), and I knew he played some games that were not considered good by most conservative standards. Yet they were being tolerated by a father who loved his son. Knowing this, I asked him how the things he allowed in his home differed from the things he felt we should allow in the church. His response still rings in my head. He told me, "I don't think the same things we allow in our homes should necessarily be allowed at church."

For me, this was telling and spoke directly to the issue of the hypocrisy, which is being perceived by the world. How can we believe that what we do outside of the Church is any less important than what we do within the walls of the church building on Sunday morning? Doesn't James remind us that freshwater and saltwater can't come from the same stream? Isn't this being double-minded? Is that not what hypocrisy is? Can we dispute that it is alive and well in most of our churches and lives? How can we have issue with a worldview that sees us in this light?

I want to say without reservation this man, who is a good man by most worldly standards and for all intents and purposes, is no different than most of us—if we are honest. He was living many different lives. He had a church life, a work life, and a home life. He was a husband, a father, a friend, a coworker, and a member of a body of believers. His life, as with that of many of us, may have looked one way on Sunday morning at church and completely different the rest of the week.

We have to realize the world sees this take place—and most people are aware of this being the case in their own lives—and nonbelievers naturally question why they should become believers. After all, the lives they see us live are often no different from their own.

Remember, the evidence of Christ in a person is what? A changed life!

If we view our lives in this way, do we have a biblical view of our lives? Of course we don't. Yet this is what is happening in many Christian churches, homes, and lives of believers everywhere, every day. Isn't it?

How can this be? Are we not sanctified or set apart? If we can say yes, we are, we know this has happened in our lives by the precious blood of Jesus. Then, why do we live lives that lack consistency? If we were aware of the need to live changed lives before the world, would its view of us and His Church be different? Surely, there is no way we can disagree here. Can we?

Our witness for Jesus, the way we represent Him, is evident and goes with us everywhere we go. Yours does, and mine does as well. The question we must ask, and should be most concerned with, is what kind of witness are we giving others? What kind of witness am I giving those around me? Only you and I can answer that question. I want us to consider that the world is watching and growing ever more disenchanted with what it sees, and the Lord is watching as well.

We cannot continue to keep out outsiders on Sunday morning and feel like it is okay to hang out with them the rest of the week. We need to feel like we should also hang out with them on Sunday morning—especially on Sunday morning.

This world is the same world all week long, and we are the same people all week long, no matter what kind of disguise we might put on. The world is watching us and knows who we really are. We may wear different faces and expect the world to see consistency when they look at us, but sadly, when they look at many of us, they see two faces and the ugliness that comes along with them.

Jesus wants us to be His followers all the time and in every phase of our lives. When we are not, we are doing damage to Him. Have you ever considered it this way? The way you and I live our lives can do damage to God. We are doing damage to His ability to be seen by those around us: those He came to save and those for whom He died. Surely, this is not acceptable to any of us. Wouldn't it be wonderful if this could not be said of any of us?

I actually had it happen to me once, and I will never forget it. My daughter, Lindsay, was about sixteen or seventeen, and we had just come from church, where the message was about living a consistent life. I said, "I hope someday, people can say that about me."

She replied, "They already can, Dad."

What a blessing. Thank you, Lindsay.

Temple-Mindedness

Where does this mind-set come from that causes us to want to keep outsiders out? Jesus said, "My house will be called a house of prayer". Matthew 21:13 HCSB May I ask, where is Jesus' house today? Doesn't He reside in each of us in the form of the Holy Spirit?

In many of the churches I have been involved with, there seems to be a reversion in many cases to what I will call "Temple-Mindedness." I say it is a reversion, because I believe it is reversing the course of the Church. It is reverting back to the original Covenant and, in the process, ignoring the New Covenant.

Because of Jesus, the Lord no longer meets with His High Priest in the Holy of Holies. He meets with all those who believe in His Son, whenever we call on Him and wherever we are. The High Priest in the Order of Melchizedek that we go through to get to God today is Jesus himself. The veil was torn in two, and the Temple has been destroyed.

From my perspective, Temple-Mindedness fosters the idea that the church itself—the building, the assembly area (sanctuary), and what it represents—is the Temple or House of the Lord. Many see the pastor as the Priest, and all things in the building must be kept holy at all cost. This is false doctrine and must be dealt with if the Church is going to complete its mission.

Remember, 1 Corinthians 6:19 HCSB, "Do you not know that your body is a sanctuary of the Holy Spirit who is in you, whom you have from God? You are not your own." Your body is a sanctuary (the Temple) of the Holy Spirit.

He doesn't reside in a building!

I understand many apply Matthew 21:13 when they consider the Church as the Temple or House of the Lord. I believe this is being taken out of context entirely. In this particular instance, Jesus is referring to the Temple, not the Church. I feel I must stress once again that the Church is not the Temple. This may be one of the most important things we as believers need to understand about the Church or the Body of Christ. It is not the Temple. It is the Body of Christ!

This idea that the Church that remains is the House of the Lord is commonplace among traditionalists, and it is off the mark entirely. Why is it important that we understand this? Because Jesus himself pointed to this as truth when He reminded us He would not leave us alone; He would send the Counselor, His Holy Spirit, who would come and dwell in us to encourage, guide, equip, and rebuke us. When you and I accepted Him, we became the place where the Holy Spirit dwells. We received in us the Holy Spirit of God, and we became the House of the Lord. He lives in each of us.

This is not my assertion alone. This is what Jesus left us with when He said in Matthew 28:20 HCSB, "And remember, I am with you always, to the end of the age."

This statement, points to Him as ever present in our lives. It brings us hope and encouragement in times of struggle.

We take Him with us everywhere we go as we give witness of Him with our very lives. We cannot do this if He lives in the building where we gather each week. As the hymn says, "We know He lives, because He lives within my heart." I am sure those who know me well may be shocked that I knew and actually quoted a hymn, but I do and I did.

Therefore, His house, His Temple, His dwelling place is not the building where we congregate each week at all. His dwelling place is in you and in me, if we believe in Him. If we can agree with this assertion, it is absolutely critical we consider what we do outside of the church and its effect on those around us. Because the truth is that we are the House of the Lord, and He is with us wherever we go. He wants us to let in outsiders. He wants us to not only let them into our church buildings on Sundays, He wants us to let them into our lives all week long. He certainly does not want us to keep them out.

Let's consider the people of God in Jesus' day. Where was the established religion of the day? We have already taken a glimpse at how the Temple was being used and what Jesus thought of that. What were God's people doing while Jesus was letting them know how He felt about them and what they were doing?

They were planning His demise, weren't they?

They were working hard to maintain the past and trying to protect their future from Him, the world, and anything else that might alter their perception of their own righteousness. Did they not see Jesus as a threat to their way of life and to everything they believed? Is it any different today?

Does not the established church of today see the world or anyone who doesn't agree with it as a threat to its beliefs and something that must be guarded against? Isn't that what refusing to change, remaining irrelevant, and keeping out outsiders really boils down to? Aren't we, as the Church, just repeating many of the same mistakes those people made? And in many cases, aren't we doing it with the same zeal that led to the crucifixion of Jesus?

So, once again, where is God in His Church?

Have you ever given thought to that line of thinking? Would we have treated Jesus any differently today than His people did when He walked the streets in the first century?

In his book Revolution published by Tyndale House Publishers in 2006 , Barna points out that if John the Baptist were alive today, we would institutionalize him. Isn't that true? We are no more likely to recognize Jesus today than they were then. Fortunately, as believers, we don't have to worry about that. He will be recognized by all the next time He comes.

The question: will it be too late?

Do we know we are missing the boat when it comes to reaching the Lost? With a little bit of honesty, I think we would all have to admit we are. Certainly, there are some who are more focused and more effective than the rest of us, but we all fall short of the mission Jesus has given us, don't we?

Is there any evidence to back up my assertion? We can see evidence of it every Sunday morning, can't we? How many churches have services every Sunday morning that never involve Lost People?

Is it because we are doing things, even if they are unintentional, that are keeping them out? Are the only new people who show up at your church ones who might just happen in? Are our churches growing? Is your church growing? Church growth in my area is from transplants (church hopping and/or church shopping), not from conversions.

Why is this? Is it for a lack of effort on our part? How do we know? We can start by asking ourselves a question: are we inviting Lost people to come with us on Sunday? Do we know any Lost people? I know you do. Let me ask you another way. Are you friends with any Lost people? If not, why not?

Again, does the church not exist to reach these Lost people? Is that not our Mission? If they are not coming to know Him, is it because we are not inviting them to know Him?

Where do we begin to identify whether this is the case for us as individuals and churches? I think we can start by being honest with ourselves. We can ask ourselves the questions I just posed. Do we know Lost people? Do we have Lost friends? How many of our churches are not representative of our communities and the cultures that surround them?

How can we tell? How many of our churches meet in neighborhoods populated by black, Hispanic, or other ethnic minority groups with no one from those groups among its members? Over time, have the communities in which these churches are located changed completely, while the churches remain unchanged. Why are we not representing the cultures and communities that surround our churches?

I have seen this phenomenon firsthand. In the middle of all this change and transition, many people who attend these churches are convinced they have no need to change, and the fact minorities are not attending their churches has nothing to do with them or says nothing about the effectiveness of their churches. The problem exists because the world is going to hell in a handbasket, and the fact these people are not attending their churches points to that.

The saddest thing we must consider is how many people attending these churches don't care if they are reaching their communities if it means they have to change what they are doing.

Is any of this striking a nerve or offending you? If what I am saying is offensive to you, I am sorry. But if what God is saying to you is offensive to you, I make no apologies for that. You can take it up with Him.

This is an area where I think we can safely say the enemy has done some of his greatest work. He has allowed man to take God's Church back to the days before Jesus. The religiosity and hierarchy that have been established since that first church in the book of Acts are starkly reminiscent of the temples of the Jews in the first century.

These same temples that did what? They tried every way they could to keep the world out of their midst—to such a degree they even had Christ crucified to preserve their place in the world. They saw themselves as the examples of godliness, and in their godliness, they missed seeing God himself as He stood right in front of them. They were so self-assured and self-absorbed that there was no convincing them otherwise. Even amid miracles such as healing and the raising of the dead, there was little or no change in their thinking. It had little effect in changing the view of the majority of those who were charged with knowing and living out God's Word. These people, who were learned and scholarly, knew right from wrong and had basically determined if you weren't in agreement with them, you were wrong. There was no debating it, and there was no way but their way.

Does any of this sound familiar? Is it any different today? The Scribes and Pharisees, Priests and Levites were the ones who knew the Scripture and came together at the appointed times to fast and to pray. They were the ones who had been charged with carrying out God's law and being prepared for the coming of the Messiah. In their minds and hearts, they were living right lives before God. Oh how they missed the mark.

What about us? Who are the Scribes and Pharisees, Priests and Levites of our day? Among believers today, how many times do you suppose we have felt justified in our indignation or judgment of someone else or some other people, group, or church?

If you are a pastor or leader in a church, I would like to ask if you are leading like Jesus led or like one of these people we have mentioned? Perhaps you are so sure of yourself and of your application of the faith you profess to have that you can't, or won't, even consider the possibility that you may be leading like one of these people. I would like to interject that you are in a very dangerous place. If you and I ever get to where we become unteachable, if we ever get to the place that we refuse to do a self-evaluation, we are of no use to God and are no different than that group of religious people in Jesus' day.

Remember, I said these people couldn't see God when He was standing right in front of them? How about us: can we? Would Jesus be welcome in our churches as He was seen in the first century? Remember the comment from Barna's book *Revolution*, if John the Baptist was here today, we would institutionalize him. Would we?

Would we welcome a man who was preaching against the established order? When someone comes into our church and starts to speak against the established order, what is your reaction? Do you tell him he can stop now? It is difficult to think about it, isn't it? As difficult as it is, it is important we learn to try. The Church, as with our lives, needs to be able to hear constructive criticism and acknowledge areas that need to be addressed. Do you do that in your churches or ministries?

Can the same attitudes that was perpetuated by these first-century men of God exist among the followers of Jesus Christ? Is there a Temple-Mindedness that exists today? Is it where you go to church? In your view, is your church the House of God? Is your pastor the priest? Is that how you see things?

Are we called to share Christ with this world, or are we called to protect His Church from it? That is the million—or by today's standards, the trillion—dollar question, isn't it? Or is it as it was in the first century? Has maintaining the status quo become so important we may miss everything that is truly important, even God Himself?

How does this happen? How do we keep it from happening to us and our churches?

First, we have to start by acknowledging it is possible—not only possible but plausible. If we are not careful, we can become so caught up in our plans that we miss His plan. We can become so consumed with our way that we forget His way.

We have to see ourselves and our lives the way we really are, not necessarily the way we hope they are. Can we do that? I think it is something each of us must deal with on an individual basis. At times, the world and those around us see us a lot more clearly than we see ourselves. This is where the whole issue of consistency again becomes so important.

How do we get so far offtrack? How do we go from people who are Lost to being accepted by Jesus? People whose hearts generally at one point or another are on fire for Him and want nothing more than to serve Him and see others come to know Him, to people who are religious and without consideration for those He came to save. It probably is different for each of us, but I can guarantee it didn't happen overnight.

As in the book The Simple Church by Thom S. Rainer and Eric Geiger published by B& H Publishing Group, we can become so consumed with ministry that we forget about the Mission altogether.

Jesus was clear in Luke 10:27 HCSB, wasn't He? Is there something hidden in the statement He gave? He answered, "'Love the Lord your God with all your heart, with all your soul, with all your strength and with all your mind; and, Love your neighbor as yourself.'" It seems pretty clear, doesn't it?

Who is your neighbor? Are we to apply this passage to the Lost? Does it not apply to those who are young both chronologically and in their faith? Are we doing this? The truth that may be forgotten by many of us is simply we are to "'Love,'" just as we have been loved.

I think if we were, and I mean the Church doing this, the Lord would be adding to our numbers daily those being saved. Once again, is that the case in your church? It is certainly not the case in my community and in the churches I have attended or served in for the last twelve years.

Sure, there are those who have found the Lord and have experienced and are experiencing spiritual growth in these churches. It's more a credit to the Lord's ability to reach into even the darkest of places and find those who are Lost.

Of course, I do not want anyone to think I have an axe to grind with a church or the Church in general. That is simply not the case. I am only trying to bring to light what I have seen and what countless books point to. You do not have to look far to find justification for these claims. In fact, look around yourself on Sunday.

As with anything, these statements are not all-encompassing, and there are and will always be exceptions. The reason we can be assured of this is that God will see His plan fulfilled in His time— with or without us. There are some local churches with large numbers that are leading people to Christ. But the statistics surrounding us continue to remain stagnant. Essentially, the number of people who attend a local church on any given Sunday never seems to change.

Why do you suppose that is, and what can we do about it? Maybe we need to start by looking inward, so we can get an idea of what we are projecting outward. How we are being seen by our world will certainly be a good indicator of how we are doing in our efforts to reach into our world. Do we like what we see when we look in the mirror? If not, you know no one else likes it either.

The Body or the Building

I have already told you about the first church my wife and I attended. It was there that I first began to experience spiritual growth. We had a sense of fellowship and belonging. Then, as with many churches, because of the Lord's blessing, a building project began.

What a waste of His blessing. Oops, I let a little personal bias shine through there.

I am sure you have been involved in one of these types of projects if you have been a believer and attended a church for any significant length of time. They are pretty typical in the way they transpire, regardless of the denomination or of the culture of the church itself.

It always starts with a blessing, as I have stated. The church is growing: people are coming. Good things are happening all around. Staff is being added. Then it happens. The inevitable comes. The church leadership gets together and decides we have to have a building to meet the demands of this blessing. It begins with prayer and is communicated by the leadership as something they believe the Lord is leading them to do to meet adequately the demands of the community around them and their growing congregations.

The next step is to raise the money to carry out God's plan for the church.

A capital campaign is started, pledges are taken, fund-raising begins, and a building committee is formed (nothing happens without a committee). After that, the focus begins to take place. I believe it is at this point we begin to stray from His plans and start to implement our own.

My first experience with such things was when a couple came to my house representing the fund-raising arm of the church's capital campaign. Ironically, this was the first time anyone from the church had visited my home.

I let them in, and we sat down. They began to share with us the church's plans for this new facility and how it was going to allow us to do so much more in the way of ministry and service to the community and to the Lord.

Bonnie and I listened intently, and though I cannot speak for her, I was blown away when they told me they wanted us to make a Faith Promise to the building fund. Then, they explained what a Faith Promise was. I was told I had to make a pledge of a certain amount of money and trust that God would provide me with this money. This money was to be above and beyond what I normally gave. Apparently, this money and my promise, along with that of other members, would be on what they would base their budget for the building. This was a completely new concept for me.

You have to remember I was about twenty-four or twenty-five years old, with a wife and young daughter.

The money we gave on Sundays was money we felt we didn't have, and now they were asking me to give more. My initial reaction was one of self-defense. I will never forget telling them, "I don't have any problem telling you I will give money and then not being able to follow through. But I have a real problem pledging to give money to the Lord and then not following through."

I think the thing that bothered me most was, even after expressing my concerns about being able to give or being willing to pledge the money, their insistence we do so anyway. It was basically communicated that everyone who was a member of the church was expected to take part in this pledge.

To this day, I feel there is no place for high-pressure sales in the Church. Does this type of behavior not feed into the worldview? To many, the Church is after their money. You can say this is not the case, that their perception is not reality, because a Faith Promise gives someone a chance to trust the Lord and see Him provide. I have no argument for this rationale—other than the fact that as a new believer, I know I was unprepared for such a consideration.

Perhaps there are many in our world today who are equally unprepared to consider such things. If we can agree that a perception of Church greed may exist, the question becomes whether it is worth the risk to ask them to make this promise.

If giving is a condition of the heart, and Jesus said it is, I think when we have a need as a church, we should make that need known to the people in our churches. Then, we should trust the Lord to speak to their hearts. I do not believe we need to tug at them ourselves.

This type of coercion fueled our own view of the cultural stigmas attached to churches and to church membership. Though we did continue to attend a while longer, we did not make the Faith Promise, and ultimately, we did not stay at the church.

By the way, just for the record, they did go on to build their building, and their church did grow. However, the pastor, the music minister, and half the congregation that was there when the project started left. However, the church did what the Lord was calling it to do. At least that is the way some would see it.

Interestingly enough, the next church we were a part of didn't have a building, and we appreciated not being involved in any sort of building project while we were there. They had other difficulties, as I have said, but the need for money or for building a facility was not one of them.

However, the little Podunk church, as I referred to it earlier, did have a building campaign when we arrived. (For those of you who were there when I was and are reading this, I want you to know that "Podunk" is meant as a term of endearment.)

Although the building campaign was not divisive, it was fraught with anxiety about issues including money, and the poor stewardship by the leadership was appalling and created all kinds of problems.

They had budgeted about $425,000, and they ended up spending about $600,000. There were many instances when there was no accounting of the money spent. Ultimately, the person who had been contracted to do the work was dismissed. The idea that we were spending our people's money without being able to account for it was something I don't think I will ever forget.

The situation in this particular church is indicative of many in the Church today. The pastor was inexperienced in such things, and so was the committee. I suppose they did the best they could, but it really boiled down to trying to get something for nothing. They never considered the cost of the tower, and they had trusted someone else to consider those cost for them. In case you are wondering, that is never a good idea.

What started as the vision of one pastor ended up being the burden for another.

My reason for going into this scenario is because this seems to happen all over the place, in church after church. Pastors, gatekeepers if you will, always seem to feel they need to be the driving force in endeavors such as these, even though many of them have absolutely no training or experience in doing so. In my experience with our denomination's DEXCOM *(District Executive Committee)*, I have sat in many meetings where a pastor had in his mind that he had to have a building. If not, he was going to lose people, because there wasn't enough room, the facilities weren't good enough, or any number of other reasons that would give credence to his need.

Each time, there always seemed to be this major sense of urgency. Each time, there wasn't enough money, and they needed a loan to carry out God's plan for their churches. I don't want you to misunderstand me. I am not beyond believing that God has communicated to a pastor, church leader, or even a leadership team through His Holy Spirit the need to grow a church and even build a facility to do so.

If it is God who has done the communicating, wouldn't He supply the people and the resources needed to accomplish His will?

This is one place that God has to be present in His Church. In a world with the economy and struggles with debt that our culture has today, the Church *must* be an example of good stewardship to its people and to the world. If we are going to combat the perceptions that we have been discussing, we cannot afford to be the example of poor stewardship.

When I have seen pastors plowing ahead in their efforts to build a building, most, if not all, of these men were godly men, serving with great conviction. But they seem to have lost sight of God in their pursuit of expanding His kingdom on earth.

Is that possible?

Can we go ahead of God and build His kingdom on our own? Obviously, the answer is no, we can't. We cannot build His kingdom without Him. However, we can definitely go off on our own and build a kingdom unto ourselves, which may see itself as representing the kingdom of God to the world or to the community around it. This kingdom, however, is lacking in the essential element: the power of God through His Holy Spirit.

Perhaps this is where today's perceptions of the Church begin. Perhaps we have, without realizing it, built a Church on the sand of our own desires and ideals, instead of building it on the "Rock": Jesus Christ. Perhaps we have become so consumed with our own vision of what the Church is that we have missed out on the consuming fire of the Holy Spirit.

Are we building kingdoms unto ourselves? Is there evidence of this in the Church today? Is there evidence of it in your church fellowship? As with so many of the questions I am asking us to consider, it comes back to looking introspectively and being honest about what we see. If you can say without a doubt that you have never experienced any of these things, you have either been blessed by experiencing a church that is Christ-centered and Christ-focused, or you are just not being honest with yourself. Remember, the only way we are going to combat the perceptions that exist about us is to be honest about what we are showing the people in our world.

To make sure we are on the same page, my contention is that the Church is the Body, *not* the building. If we can agree this is true, we must believe if God's plan is to prosper our ministries and to build and grow His Church, He will do so. And the gates of hell will not be able to stand against it!

I am not suggesting it is always wrong to move ahead when we feel the Lord is prompting us to do so. I am one of those most likely to do just that. What I am suggesting is that we should not move ahead of God into areas we have not been equipped to move into at all. And we certainly should not do so ahead of Him.

We must always be aware that when our focus becomes anything other than Jesus, we have erred and need to rethink what it is we are trying to do and why we are trying to do it.

In my limited experience, I have seen many churches built, many loans taken out, and many congregations fall apart as an end result. Is there a correlation? In my opinion, there is undoubtedly such a correlation.

Each time a building fund becomes a constant topic, many people become disillusioned with the purpose of the church. For many, it tends to feed that perception the Church just wants my money.

Do you hear what I am saying?

When we lose sight of our purpose, which is His Mission, we begin to lose control of the very ministry with which He entrusted us. If you have been in a church leadership capacity for any length of time, it is hard to disagree with what I say.

If you have been involved in a building project, everything becomes about the building program, doesn't it? The announcements become about giving to the building fund and the status of the plans or construction. Our prayers become about the building committee, permits, for the need for giving to increase, the status of the loan, the state of construction, and on and on.

Our sermons begin to be filled with anecdotes about the experiences we are having and the struggles with contractors or authorities having jurisdiction. It is amazing, but everything begins to revolve around this project. Even with our best intentions, this becomes the case. Even when we feel we haven't lost sight of Him or of what is important, we have to admit the importance of these projects becomes our number-one priority.

All the while, we begin to see every problem or hindrance placed in front of us as being put there by the enemy. We begin to ask the Lord to remove these things we perceive as obstacles, and we pray for His protection from the enemy. The possibility the Lord Himself has placed some of these obstacles in front of us, because we are already moving too fast or not in the direction He would have us go is almost never considered. If the final result of these endeavors is division, or the total collapse of a ministry, isn't it quite possible it is a result of us subverting His plan?

How does this happen to us, our churches, and our ministries? How do we start out with our hearts and minds focused on serving God and carrying out His Mission and end up with hearts and minds filled with anxiety about a building that will eventually return to the dust from which it came?

I believe it happens the same way to all of us. It is the same thing I am guilty of in many cases. We have a plan, and we expect the Lord to align His plans with ours. When that doesn't happen, we are sure it is the enemy, and we do everything we can to move our plan forward, while all the while, God is telling and showing us we need to stand still and wait.

Do you do that?

Do you make a plan and then seek God's help? I can say in all honesty and without reservation that I have and I do. Unfortunately for me, it has been my history more times than not. It is something I am aware of in my character, and it is something that I am working to improve.

Why do you suppose we do these things? What causes us to move ahead of God? I am sure we can come up with all kinds of reasons and justifications. At least I know I can. For me, it is simply a matter of an unwillingness to be patient. Really, it is because the Lord just doesn't move fast enough for me in my life and certainly in areas of ministry in which I have served. For me, this has been and continues to be a problem.

Should we move ahead of Him? Or should we seek first His kingdom and His righteousness?

I am not trying to over-spiritualize this matter. I am only trying to point out that we have a ready, willing, and able God, who will lead us if we allow Him. Too many times, we move out on our own.

Do we want the world to see the followers of Jesus Christ leading His Church our way, or do you suppose their view of us would be different if He were leading His Church, His Way?

Unfortunately, instead of waiting and allowing Him to lead us, many of us move ahead in spite of His plan. What we find at the end of our pursuit, and in most cases what has transpired, was not His plan at all. It probably wasn't even the plan we had worked so hard to carry out.

Instead of doing this, shouldn't we be praying for the Lord to allow His Will to be done in our plans and then expect it to be done and accept what is done. I know that it is hard to do. I have never said I have been able to accomplish all the things I know I should be doing. But my hope is that at least I will learn from my mistakes and not repeat them.

Remember Albert Einstein's definition of insanity: "Insanity" is repeating the same things over and over and expecting to have a different result. Regarding this particular subject, I think it is safe to say the world may see us as a little insane, as we continue to trip and stumble over many of the same things over and over again.

We have to get back to the reality that the Church is His, and it is His Body, not the building. When we begin to see things this way and to function as such, God will care for His Body as He has promised.

Pastor of All Trades

O n many occasions and in no uncertain terms, I have been reminded by overseers, pastors, and other leaders that the Church is not a business. This has been said during meetings with those in leadership positions on both the local level and the regional level.

Of course, I cannot know the true intention of those types of comments, since I have never asked if they were indeed directed at me or whether they were intended for my benefit. However, one thing that has always been true about this statement is that none of the people who have made it to me have been businesspeople. They are either lower-tier employees of a company or professional clergy. Each time the statement is made, I listen to the proclamation and defer my opinion for another time.

Perhaps now is that time.

Let's begin with the statement, the Church is not a business. It is also not a temple or a building. The Church is the Body of Christ.

The problem is that the church, in my experience, is guided by the principles of business. Churches are incorporated, which means they have officers and articles of incorporation. They have policies and procedures under which they operate. They file for federal tax ID numbers.

It sounds like a business to me. Not only to me but to the government, who issues them their 501(c)(3) status as a not-for-profit business. So, strictly for clarification, the church established by man, under the law that operates in America today, is a business.

If you notice, I said established by man. God's Church is not a business; nor is it a Temple or a building. It is the Body of Christ. The problem is that we have adopted all the rules of a business in order to function under the laws of our respective states, and we have not applied the principles of a business to our structures.

In many cases, the people who have taken on the responsibility of administrating these business enterprises do not understand these rules and principles, and yet, they function in capacities within the church that require them to have this knowledge. Why is this?

This brings me to a very interesting point regarding those in leadership in many churches today. The Church is indeed not prepared to operate as a business. This is why I have titled this section "Pastor of All Trades."

These people are inclined to fill in the gap wherever and whenever they see the need. Some of this is because they feel no one else will. Some of it is because they feel no one else can, and some of it may be because they simply feel they are supposed to. I am inclined to believe the latter is more likely the case.

In the churches where I have been involved, the pastor is expected and to be a pastor of all trades. Because of this expectation, they feel they have no choice but to do things they are not equipped to do. If they don't do this for some reason, many seem to think they are delegating authority they have been called to have. I have been ashamed to see otherwise godly men struggle to do the things God has not equipped them to do and things that He certainly has not called them to do. Many will persist in plowing ahead, regardless of the depth of their inability to function within the capacity in which they are trying to function.

Again, we reflect back to the business model.

In business, we look for people who are gifted and equipped to do the things we are not necessarily gifted or equipped to do or that we cannot necessarily spend our time doing if our organization is going to function as it is intended. We often realize the very survival of our organizations depends on delegating responsibilities to those best equipped to handle them. Thereby, we create a system within our structure that functions at the peak of its abilities.

Paul said the Church is the Body of Christ. I love the simplicity of God's truth. It works for someone as simple as me.

If you are a pastor, please take a moment and consider what I am proposing. Please understand, it is not my intention to take a shot at you. I have sat in your chair and understand the stresses that are placed on you. I am certain some of you would say that since I have always been a businessman, even when serving in the capacity of a pastor, I truly do not understand what I am talking about. If that is your position, I respect it and ask your indulgence for the next few moments.

One thing I can honestly say is when I have held the positions of pastor and businessman at the same time, I have had to learn to allow those I placed in positions of leadership to lead. And at least in my experience, they have become better leaders because of it. Discipleship doesn't mean creating Mini Mes, does it? Doesn't it mean helping people become followers of Jesus? If each of these people represents a part of the Body of Christ, aren't they equipped by Him to perform at some level or within some capacity?

In our effort to maximize the volunteer forces available to us, I think we often try to re-create these volunteer forces into what we think they should be and not necessarily what God created them to be. Maybe you have not experienced this in your fellowship, but it is taking place in many.

Interestingly enough, in a position that is always hoping for more servants, many pastors will not allow others to serve without their direct oversight. This willingness to micromanage is very common and perhaps evidence of an insecurity that may exist. This is a shame for the pastor and for those willing and trying to serve. Micromanaging can be stifling to those who desire to serve.

There has to be a point in our lives as leaders, whether in the ministry or in business, when we realize we cannot do everything well, nor should we. Since we all know the Church is the Body of Christ, we should be willing to allow it to function as such and to acknowledge that Christ—not us—is the head of the Church. This is true whether we are the pastor or an overseer. This, I believe, will be both transformational and freeing when we apply it to our churches or ministries.

I spent many years in business, believing I was the best at what I do and that no one could do it the way I wanted it done. I was wrong on both accounts. Although I certainly have gifts for certain things, over time, I discovered there are others who are also gifted, in many cases more so than I. At first, it was a little disconcerting. But then I realized this was not a threat to me; this was an opportunity for me to allow someone else to do what the Lord had gifted him to do, and in the long run, everyone involved benefited.

The success of any organization hinges on our ability to maximize our potential. We can only do this when we allow others to reach theirs. If you are a pastor or overseer of a ministry or a church, I would like you to ask yourself if you are doing these things. Are you micromanaging others? Are you stifling their creativity? Are you insecure as a leader? If you answer yes to any of those questions, I want you to know you can change what you're doing. When you do, you will free yourself and your organization to reach the fullness God has planned. The result will be a Body that functions like the wondrous creation it is.

For my friends who are pastors I do not mean for my writing to have venom. If you are one of these men, you will know to what I refer. If not, please just believe that is not my intent.

I would like us to consider the primary difference between the function of a church organization and the function of a business. You could say simply one is designed and purposed with the task of making money, and the other is designed and purposed with the task of making Disciples. One is earthly minded, and one is kingdom minded. Both of these statements can be true. But both of these organizations can become the same thing. A business can be used to make disciples, can't it? And unfortunately, a church can be used to make money.

The former, a business when being used to make disciples, is a wonderful thing, and as a Christian business owner, I strive to do just that: to make disciples even in the midst of our pursuit of income. In the latter, the church is being used to make money, nothing is seen as more reprehensible. Let's pray that this view, which many in the world has of the Church, is based on a misconception.

For me, there is another significant difference between the two.

Secular organizations (businesses) have management structures in which people are generally recruited for a particular position and to perform a particular task.

After being recruited and going through a process of interviews and evaluations, they are hired because of their strengths, aptitudes, or gifts, which were identified and seen as compatible with the needs and the direction of the organization. Then, they are given the resources necessary to carry out their task and the encouragement and empowerment to do so, with the hope the end result will be a successful undertaking, one mutually beneficial to everyone involved.

Some of you may be thinking these people get paid for what they do, and those who serve in the church are volunteers who do not get paid. I have no argument with your dispute. I would only say that it has been my experience that when people are serving or volunteering, they have a vested interest that, in many cases eclipses that of a paycheck. They are serving the Living God, and no secular business or organization can compete with that. They serve with passion and conviction when they serve their Lord. They are giving of themselves, and their reward is in knowing that the glory goes to Him.

In the Church, or at least in the churches I have been witness to, it tends to be completely different. First of all, there really isn't much discipleship taking place, even though making disciples might even be in their mission statement. When there is a need to fill a position, the pastor or some other leader simply picks someone out of the congregation and asks him if he would like to serve in a particular capacity. This is usually based on a perceived level of spiritual maturity, observed from a casual relationship at best.

The passages from Timothy and Titus concerning the qualifications for an overseer are given some consideration and usually loosely applied. After one has agreed to serve, the areas he begins to oversee are the usually ones he feels called to, not necessarily the ones he is called to by God and not necessarily the ones for which he has been equipped.

As a point of reference, and as most people can attest, liking to sing does not mean you are gifted in music. Consequently, if you like to talk, it does not mean you are gifted in preaching or teaching. Many seem to feel called to these two areas, even though they may not possess the gifts or the skills necessary to be fruitful in these particular areas of ministry. These are God-given gifts and skills; they are not manmade, and quite honestly, you either have them or you don't.

I had a music leader tell me once, when I objected to a certain person singing, that he really had a heart for singing. My contention was if his heart for singing causes the entire church to lose the heart of worship, it is not of God. To some, I am sure this may sound harsh. But if we are going to function as the Body of Christ, we must operate together in the areas in which we have been gifted and equipped to operate. If not, we will not be functioning as we were created to operate.

In the Church, as in the world, leaders are born; they are not made.

Try though someone might, you either have a particular gift or you don't. Unfortunately, many view themselves as a leader, because they have been placed in a position of leadership, even though they have no ability to lead and no one is following. No other leaders are following them.

The reason for my last statement is I believe, and many contemporary teachers on leadership agree, "Leaders follow leaders, not followers." John Maxwell said it best in his book the 21 Irrefutable Laws of Leadership by Thomas Nelson publishing. Law number two, the Law of Influence.: "He who thinks he leads, but has no followers, is only taking a walk."

Herein lies a major problem for the church and another thing that clearly points to the truth in the statement that the Church is not a business. Once you have placed someone who has volunteered to serve in an area they feel called to, it is very difficult to remove them without doing harm. You have legitimized their belief in themselves, and the level of maturity perceived in them may not be quite as evident when it comes to being told it doesn't appear they are gifted to serve in this area. In many cases, the idea of serving in a leadership capacity within the church is seen as a validation of spiritual maturity. Though this certainly can be true, it often points to the obvious immaturity that had not been seen until they were asked to step down.

Those who are serving in these areas often begin to see themselves worthy of the position and far more capable than they really are. Jesus' words in Matthew 23:11 spoke directly against this type of self-assurance: "The greatest among you will be your servant." The privilege of serving God in His Church, and it is a privilege, is one that should always humble us. My belief is if you feel you should be an overseer, most likely you should not.

I know many of you are thinking of the passage from 1 Timothy 3:1: "Here is a trustworthy saying: If anyone sets his heart on being an overseer, he desires a noble task." I believe this is true precisely as it is written. If someone sets his heart on serving in this way, he desires a noble task. It does not mean he sees himself worthy of it and seeks it out. As with humility, the qualifications of an overseer are seen in us by others, not ourselves.

Pastors, when you feel like you have to do everything or fill every positional need in the church you have been called to serve, if you find yourself desiring to or believing you have to do everything in a church, please consider there is usually fallout. Even as I write this, I know there are many of you who will continue to feel the need to do just.

If we are the Body, it may be time we start to function as one and allow the other parts of the body to function in the areas in which they were created to function.

Let's try and be the pastor of but one trade.

Be Transformed,
Not Conformed

Pastor Larry Mayer of Life Church in Wellington, FL said, "In the passage Romans 12: 2, they have put a period after the word conform, and they have stopped there."

Of course, we all know this passage and understand it is about our being set apart (sanctified) as Christians. Romans 12:1–2 HCSB: "1 Therefore, brothers, by the mercies of God, I urge you to present your bodies as a living sacrifice, holy and pleasing to God; this is your spiritual worship. Do not be conformed to this age, but be transformed by the renewing of your mind, so that you may discern what is the good, pleasing, and perfect will of God."

To what are we no longer to conform? It says "this age," doesn't it? Does that mean we are not to be like the world? Yes it does—when it comes to those areas of our lives from which we have been set apart. But we have to be careful. It doesn't mean we are to live in such a way that the world doesn't want to associate with us. First Peter 1:14 HCSB points out we are not to conform to the desires of our former ignorance: "As obedient children, do not be conformed to the desires of your former ignorance."

Nonconformity is not setting ourselves apart from the world. It is about God, setting us apart from our former ignorance or from the way we lived before we accepted Jesus. It is about being set apart for service and the transforming that takes place with the renewing of our minds. Renewing our minds starts with changing them. We choose to focus on God and His plan instead of ourselves and what we feel is important.

To many, it seems the understanding of sanctification or being set apart means we have been removed from the world. Are we to hold up in our buildings and deem the world unworthy of our involvement? How ironic is it that Jesus came to save this world and the perception that is given by many is that it has no value. How many times have you spoken with a mature believer who will tell you how bad the world is today and how we have to keep ourselves from being involved in the things of this world and not allow them to enter the church.

The word many like to throw around when talking about the state of the world is "carnal." My contention is the world is not carnal, it is mankind outside of Jesus Christ. And it is this carnal group of people He came and died for: people just like you and me. Sorry.

It may be this fear of conformity that shackles the Church the most. Could this be the greatest fear in the traditional Church today? Has the understanding of our being set apart by our faith in Christ been replaced with the attitude of being set apart from the world?

I am not suggesting we embrace all the relativistic thinking of our postmodern culture. I am suggesting that we embrace the thinking of Jesus, who, though not tolerant of sin, recognized the need to love the sinner.

It would appear that many have forgotten that accepting Jesus doesn't make you sin-free. It makes you forgiven for the sins you have committed and will commit.

Maintaining the sanctity of the church building is of paramount importance to traditional churchgoers. The thought of things such as short pants, flip-flops, coffee, and preaching without a tie or jacket are considered distasteful to the point that many are incapable of worshipping God because of what they see as disrespectful, if not heretical.

My friend Dave reminds me that we have to be careful not to be militant on either extreme. It has been wise counsel for someone like me, who might tend to go too far the other way. It is an amazing thing about the pendulum: it always seems to swing too far, no matter the direction.

The question that continues to resound in my heart is where is the redeeming power of God in this type of thinking? If God meant to separate us from the world completely, why did He leave us here and direct us to go into the world and preach His Gospel? Surely, the intent was that we are in the world, and I am certain that means directly and literally. The common cry is that we are in the world, not of the world. You get no argument from me on that issue. The question is how are we in the world? Does the world see the Church as a lighthouse, which would be used to point others to Jesus and give guidance and direction, or as a spotlight to be used to interrogate and bring down judgment on everyone who doesn't share our viewpoint? If our Lord and Savior did not come to judge the Lost, how do we feel it has become our responsibility to do so?

In many ways, I feel so blessed to not have grown up in the Church. I am not encumbered by any of the traditions that seem so divisive to me. I don't really care about the structure of the service as the traditionalist might. I am not overly moved by a particular hymn any more than I might be by a chorus or other, more recent, style of music or worship. I truly believe because of where I have been in my life, I have always felt privileged to serve in capacities such as a pastor or (elder) overseer. I really have never thought of myself, as being worthy of these opportunities of service or someone else as being less worthy than I am to serve in a similar capacity. I only hope it stays this way. Unfortunately, this way of thinking is commonplace among traditionalists and is usually communicated by those who would consider themselves to be the spiritually mature of the Church.

Along with this perception is the attitude that if we allow worldliness to creep into the Church, it will defile God's Temple. My fear is that this attitude itself is one of worldliness. Isn't it an attitude of judgment and self-righteousness? We could certainly agree it should be found in and would be more appropriate in the world than in the Church. The irony is that each of us came from this same world from which many would protect God and His Church. Apparently, the same rules do not apply to others that applied to us.

For me, this reeks of piousness and self-righteousness.

Isn't this exactly what Jesus spoke against in Matthew 3:7 HCSB, where he referred to the Pharisees and Sadducees as a, "Brood of Vipers"? Weren't these people representative of the spiritually mature? Isn't this exactly why He came to establish a New Covenant?

In Hebrews 8:13 HCSB, we are reminded that by saying a "New Covenant," He has declared the first is old. And what is old and aging is about to disappear. Wasn't that because man could not live up to the law established by God under the first covenant?

My fear is that we have become so caught up in our religion that we have forgotten our relationship. For many, the joy of knowing Jesus has become the burden of maintaining the sanctity of a perception or a building. The idea that it is more important to sing hymns and say the doxology than to reach the next generation for Jesus is certainly shameful, if not sinful.

The next question for me is one I feel needs great consideration from the Church of Jesus Christ today. Have we become so afraid of the sins of the world that we have forgotten the sinners? Are we so caught up in our own religious experience that we have forgotten we, too, were saved from the same sins we fear will tarnish the Church? The truth is that the same sins we say we are protecting the Church from exist within its walls as commonly as they do outside them. Though this statement is certainly sad, all the latest research and statistics bear it out. It is this idea that prompted the title for this book, Where Is God in His Church?

There are so many examples of this in my experience, and I truly believe each time a barrier is created to secure the Temple, it blocks the door to the church and keeps out the world. Barriers such as styles of worship and dress, intolerance of cultural differences, ethnicity, socioeconomic status and political views are clearly dividing God's Church. All the while, the Church speaks to the world about the unity of the Body of Christ. It is this inconsistency that leads to many of the perceptions we have discussed.

Clearly, this inconsistency can be seen as false doctrine or bad theology and has to be corrected. If not, we are doomed to repeat the same mistakes of those who yelled, "Crucify," him when the Lord was here the first time.

This is not God's plan for His Church. We have either thwarted His plan or devised our own. Either way, the world is watching, and clearly, they do not like what they see.

The Homeless Man

As I walked into church one Sunday morning, I saw a bicycle leaning against the wall. It was loaded and had about everything one could imagine hanging on it. A man stood just inside the church door. He was dirty and didn't smell too good. Just from his appearance, I assumed he was homeless. I walked up to him, introduced myself, and shook his hand. I told him if he liked, he could go on in and have a seat, and church would begin in about fifteen minutes. I watched him meander in and walk all the way up the aisle and sit in the front row. Seeing that, I knew he wasn't a regular attendee of any church, because as every pastor can attest, no one ever sits in the front row.

As I stood in the foyer of the church, greeting people as they entered in that morning, a man who was a longtime member of this congregation approached me to ask about someone he had noticed sitting in the front row of the church.

This Christ Follower's question to me was a simple one. He asked very bluntly, "John, what is that man doing here?" As you might be astonished by the abruptness of this question, I want you to realize that the man he was referring to was dirty and he smelled, and this was a church that had the same basic group of people every week for the ten years I had been attending and serving there. Any new person would draw attention in this church, and this man certainly caught the eye of everyone. Not only did his presence draw attention, his actual appearance certainly did. It created concern for some, especially for this particular man.

I am sure many of you may be shocked by the fact that someone would ask such a question, and there were many there who would have been shocked as well. I am also certain there are just as many who would really want to ask the same question but wouldn't, because you wouldn't want to be thought less of for asking it. Many of you have already considered the wrong that is associated with this type of question. You may also be thinking, this would never happen in my church.

What makes you so sure this question wouldn't be asked where you go to church? Would this man be seen as a person loved by God and welcomed with open arms? It is a legitimate question, isn't it?

The politically correct answer in the year 2010, even in the church, is to say, "Of course, he would be welcomed here. Everyone is welcome here." The answer may be easy to give, but the follow-through is a whole different story, isn't it? Maybe you still think it is an easy answer for you and your church. If that is so, praise the Lord. But if not, don't beat yourself up. You are not alone.

Let's take this situation a step further.

What if this man sat by you, your family, or your teenage daughter? Would he still be welcome? I know the question is hypothetical, and your answer is as well. I am just trying to get us to the point where we can see the hypocrisy we are demonstrating to the world if this is a possibility in our churches.

We have to keep in mind that the model is Jesus, and we know this is precisely the kind of man He came to save. This is precisely the kind of person you and I were to God before we accepted Jesus. We were lost and filthy in our sinful state. The answer to the question becomes a lot more difficult as we become personally involved, doesn't it?

One of my hopes in writing this book is that we can start to see some these issues as real and personal issues facing us as a Church and as individual believers. These issues are not abstract ones belonging to someone else. They are our issues, and they are representative of how the Church is viewed by the world. If we accomplish nothing other than to see this as a possibility and an affront to God, maybe we can start to overcome these issues. The results will be changed perceptions that may lead to a revival in our churches and an outpouring of the Holy Spirit in our world. Perhaps, we can start living as the Body of Christ and be willing to accept the responsibility for what occurs within that body.

In case you are wondering, my response to the man who asked the question was, "Maybe he is here, looking for Jesus. Do you think he might be able to find Him here?" The man just looked at me and walked away.

Do you think he could find Jesus where you attend church?

Was this man's question wrong? Perhaps not, but it points out one clear example of the church keeping out the world, even to the point of questioning why they would be there in the first place.

I am not trying to pass judgment on anyone. I am not throwing the man who asked the question, "What is he doing here?" under the bus. I just want us to consider the possibility that we have grown accustomed to keeping the world out of our churches. We have gotten so used to the fact that the Church is for people who look like us, act like us, and generally speak like us. Anyone who is different than we are may be seen by us as a genuine cause for concern.

Once again, the world's view, or perception—their reality as discussed—can be easily seen if we choose to look.

The World Is Watching

I hope we agree the world has a certain perspective of the Church, and that perspective or viewpoint has led them to a certain perception of reality regarding the Church in general and Christians in particular.

We surely must admit the world is watching us. Do the stories I have shared to this point not give credence to what they say their perception of the Church is? Or if you say it does not give credence to their viewpoint, can we at least agree it gives evidence to what they claim to see, even if we are only willing to say these are a few isolated cases?

Is there an attitude of judgment or a sense of superiority in the Church today? If so, where does this come from and what is causing it? Is this how the Church is reacting to the world? Have we become so disenchanted with the world that we detest it and, therefore, detest those who are in it and do not belong to Him? Oh, I hope not.

The one thing that has always blessed me about my Lord is His willingness to see me as worthy of His sacrifice, all the while knowing how wretched I can be. Does having a hope that comes from knowing and trusting in Jesus for our salvation give us a right to deem others unfit? Do we have an air of superiority? Are we judging the world and the Lost as beyond saving? Surely, this cannot be the case, can it? For something even more sobering for me, I would ask, isn't this how the religious elite of Jesus' day reacted to Him and to the world of their day? Did they not use their position and places of religious hierarchy to look down on those they considered beneath them?

Maybe we can say this is not the way it is in our case, and the stories I have shared are isolated and not representative of the Church as a whole. Maybe you will say, "The Church does a lot of good and helps a lot of people, and the good far outweighs these few isolated incidents." Again, is this how Jesus would see it, or would He remind us of the need to, "Love our neighbors as ourselves"? Would He not say, "A little yeast will spoil the whole loaf"?

I am not going to give you the answer to these questions. Instead, I am going to encourage you to ask Him yourself. I believe He will provide you with an unequivocal answer. I also suggest you remember one "ah shoot," outweighs a thousand "at-a-boys!"

Do you ever wonder if perhaps we have grown so jaded and calloused in our pursuit of spirituality that we have lost the Spirit completely? Have we become so ministry-minded that we are of no earthly good? My concern in asking this question is for the Body of Christ: the Church. My concern is how all of this reflects on Jesus. Isn't that what really matters?

If the Holy Spirit is with us, we have failed to hear Him, as He is no doubt telling us to share Christ with everyone we can, everywhere we can, and anytime we can, in Jerusalem, Judea, Samaria, and to the ends of the earth. This would certainly include those who are different than we are.

The sad reality is this is no different than the religious elite of Jesus' day. As a man who truly loves the book of Ecclesiastes, I will quote Solomon as he reminds us in Ecclesiastes 1:9 HCSB, "There is nothing new under the Sun." What is being done has been done before. History does repeat itself for those of us who do not learn from it.

It may be uncomfortable to think of ourselves in this way, but how sad is it if that is the very way we are being perceived by the world? I find it very disturbing to consider today's Church in that light. Unless you are involved in a church that is doing some serious introspective soul-searching, you are most likely a part of this mind-set. I would even assert that some who are reading this are already contemplating judgment on me for being so willing to disparage the Church. Perhaps you will refuse to read further, because you do not appreciate the way you perceive my intent. As before, if I have offended anyone, I am sorry, but if the Lord is offending you, so be it.

You know I am speaking to myself and looking at my own life as I make statements about the Church in our world today. The things I refer to are based on my own experiences and took place in churches I have been a part of and in areas of ministry I have overseen.

I am no different than most of you. When I think that the world is watching me, it is unnerving as I consider my actions, my attitudes, and even my choice of words, especially when I think about how they might reflect on their view of Jesus. What is astonishing to me is when I have had opportunity to pose many of these questions to people in the churches I have mentioned, they have had no problem answering with confidence that they believe their lives would reflect favorably on Christ.

If you share that belief, God bless you, and keep up the good work. If not, I hope you will join me in praying the Lord will open our eyes and our hearts to the areas we have become blind to, and we will genuinely begin to see.

If we can agree that the world is watching, hopefully we can say our goal is to let them see Jesus in us.

Reflecting Jesus

Exemplify Jesus

Where do we go from here, and how can we address this problem that we face as we become more and more aware that the world is watching us?

For the Church today, as for me, we must start by doing something I have told many people whom I have interviewed for a job. I believe it is a simple yet sound philosophy. Sometimes, in order to move forward, we must take a step back. To improve our situation, we need to redirect our path and be willing to take the necessary steps to do that.

This certainly is something the Church needs to consider at this particular point in its history. If we are going to become a Mission-minded, Christ-centered, Church that exemplifies Jesus and makes a difference in our world, we need to start by doing just that: we need to start by exemplifying Jesus. If we can conclude that exemplifying Jesus is where we need to start, we can begin by looking at His life.

Reading about His early childhood in Luke 2:49 HCSB, we are told He knew when He stayed behind at the Temple as His parents left Jerusalem and came back after three days searching for Him, "He had to be in His Father's House."

I would like us to consider His determination in the face of the worst kind of odds. Jesus had, as we need to have, a single-minded

115

focus (a pure heart), on the Father and the Mission He had been given. He was undeterred in His pursuit of that Mission. Jesus was a revolutionary man. His message was one of love, mercy, and forgiveness. It was also a message of obedience, steadfastness, and courage in the face of a hostile world. He defied the established order, which incensed the religious elite toward Him. His boldness and courage in the face of those who would see Him dead was awe-inspiring. His willingness to challenge the religious establishment of the day gives testimony to His resolve in carrying out His Father's plan. He was, and still is, countercultural. He spoke with authority and lived with conviction. He was admired by many and hated by many more. All the while, He was willing to lay down His life for each of them and for each of us.

Have you ever thought about your life in comparison to His? The term "Christian" actually means "Little Christ." Does that name fit you? Would people know we are His disciples just by watching our lives?

If we consider ourselves to be His disciples or His followers, are we willing to carry out His plan with that same single-minded focus that He lived out so powerfully and left behind as the example for us to follow?

What if in order to do this, if exemplifying Jesus starts by rocking everything we see as important and causes us to see a new paradigm? Are we willing to become the hands and feet of Christ to a lost and dying world? Can you and I become teachable again?

Corporately, we need to begin as the first church began: with a heart filled with love for Him and love for others. This first church, the church that was established in the book of Acts, was not a Temple-minded church. Quite the contrary. It met in homes. It didn't have or even need a building or a program, a praise team, or even a pastoral staff. This church had everything it needed, because it was dependent on Christ and on each other. Can you imagine being a part of such a fellowship? Perhaps you are, and if so, be thankful for that, as most of us are a part or a shadow of such a church.

Acts 2:45-47 HCSB tells us that in this church, "they sold their possessions and property and distributed the proceeds to all, as anyone had a need. And every day they devoted themselves to meeting together in the temple complex, and broke bread from house to house. They ate their food with gladness and simplicity of heart, praising God and having favor with all the people." The results of this church were that the Lord added daily to their number those who were being saved. If you consider your church to be like this one, I would ask you if the Lord is adding to your numbers daily those who are being saved. If not, I want us to consider why not.

What is missing from our fellowship that was present in that first church? I am afraid the answer may very well be a love for God and for each other. Perhaps in our effort to establish denominations and doctrines and build buildings to allow us to have programs and activities, we have forgotten what those people of the first-century church knew for certain: the joy that comes from a relationship with Jesus and with one another.

Maybe we have become so ministry-minded we are of no earthly good.

Can it be that the Church, the body of Christ, is no longer invoking the power of the love of God and for one another? What about the Holy Spirit? Is He alive and active in our churches? Is the problem simply because we have forgotten our reason for being, our first love?

How wonderful would it be if our fellowships experienced today what that first church experienced? One of the beauties of the Christian experience is that it is never too late. We can repent, be forgiven, and refocus ourselves on the Mission Jesus gave us and, once again, become that thing that draws people to Him.

This can happen again in God's Church, but first we have to remember that the Temple was destroyed, and the Great High Priest is Jesus.

Our Reflection

I would challenge you to consider whether you are confident that your life reflects well on Jesus. Are you sure this is the view those who know you would have? Or better yet, those who only have limited contact with you? What do you think that they would say? What about those in our lives outside of the church? Would they say they see Jesus in us? Would they say they see Him in you?

Do you think most of us would be willing to hear their answer, or would we be like Jack Nicholson said when he challenged Tom Cruise in the movie *A Few Good Men,* "You can't handle the truth"?

If our lives reflect Him well, the world's view of the Church would most certainly be perceived differently. Do you ever wonder about this? Do you want to know the answer to that question?

I am afraid that when we see ourselves as the model of spirituality, we are most certainly not. It is not unlike the comment made earlier concerning "overseers." When someone asks us if we are humble and our answer is yes, we are not. Our humility, as with our reflection of Jesus, will be something that others see in us, not something we see in ourselves.

When I had this particular discussion with Brad, one of my brothers-in-law, recently, he wasn't in complete agreement with my assertion. He pointed out that you may be able to see yourself as humble if you are good at something, like playing ball or another area where you know you are gifted, and you respond by saying no, or, "I'm not sure." His point was that you are demonstrating humility.

My response to him was that not being arrogant by saying you are good at something is still not the same as being humble. The easy way to prove my point is to think of someone you see humility in and ask yourself if you see yourself like that. I don't believe you will, and if you do, you are definitely not humble. Maybe I am demonstrating my own lack of humility when I tell you this. The same thing can be said of the way we reflect Jesus. Think about someone in whom you see Jesus. Do you see that in yourself?

For many believers today, it is almost impossible to consider they may not be such great witnesses for Jesus or that their church may not be the welcoming and hospitable place they believe it is. No matter how we slice it, we understand why the perception of the Church is what it is. I am not sure which of these situations is the saddest. Is it worse to not be able to see the need for improvement in our witness for Jesus, or to see it and not care enough to change it?

Does any of this ring true for you or for your church? Does it matter to you? If it does matter, does it matter enough to change the way you do things?

I don't want to sound authoritative here, but if you can say that the things I am discussing remind you of someone other than yourself or someplace other than the place you worship, chances are you are suffering from the same disease.

Our reflection of Jesus may very well be the only thing someone ever sees in his search for spirituality. How sad will it be if what one sees in us and our churches is what leads him to look elsewhere?

The Influence of Our Culture

The denomination I am a part of and licensed through, the Christian and Missionary Alliance (CMA), has a history of amazing missionary work all over the world. Its efforts in carrying out the Great Commission is second to none. It has a sense of identity in that effort and is larger around the world than it is here in America.

Its doctrinal positions on Jesus Christ being, Our Savior, Our Sanctifier, Our Healer, and Our Coming King are sound, and its core beliefs are based on a biblical worldview. Its desire to see all those who don't know Jesus be given the opportunity is sincere and heartfelt.

It was started as a Holy Spirit–led fellowship, not a denomination, by A. B. Simpson in direct response to a church he was pastoring. That church was not welcoming of those who were seen as lesser people by the core members of this wealthy church. He would not be a part of something trying to keep out the world. By doing so, it hindered the spreading of the Gospel. Simpson left that church to start a fellowship with a focus on uniting believers of all denominations to reach the world for Jesus.

What a demonstration of what it means to follow Jesus. Sadly, as this group has grown, it has lost sight of that beginning. The result of this lost vision are churches rooted in the past and struggling to survive in today's world. In many cases, these churches are dying. They are experiencing a physical death, because there is no infusion of life in their congregations. No young people are coming, or they are not staying when they reach the place in their own lives where they can choose to go elsewhere.

This is a sad indictment, because the churches I have personally been involved with do not see this as having anything to do with them. Nor do they understand why this is happening. They don't see themselves as irrelevant. They see themselves as not forsaking the past in order to reach the present. They see themselves, doing as Paul states in 1 Corinthians 11:2 HCSB, as holding on to traditions just as I passed them to you . This has caused stagnated attendance and in most cases, a steady decline. In their effort to reach the ends of the earth, they have forgotten about Jerusalem, Judea, and Samaria. They have closed their doors to the world and lost their social significance.

The fear of being influenced by our culture is real in these particular churches. Styles are more important than substance, conformity is expected, and nonconformity is unacceptable. Anything less than what has been done in the past is not welcome.

One of the real shames in these types of churches is that the leadership uses the elderly in the congregation as the excuse for not changing, thereby fulfilling their own desire to see the church remain as it was when they were young. They are meeting their personal needs and the needs of the group of people among them that share their same viewpoint.

They have taken the idea of a fellowship of believers and limited it to their fellowship. Are they wrong in their desire to have a fellowship that serves them? Perhaps not, but is that the purpose of the Church?

DOCTRINE OR DOGMA

I have expressed the belief that the doctrine of the CMA is sound. However, for many in leadership roles and for many who have attended these churches for generations, I am afraid this doctrine has turned to dogma.

How can I make this statement? Well, simply by pointing to a doctrine that proclaims Christ as Our Savior, Our Sanctifier, Our Healer, and Our Coming King and then looking at churches that do not demonstrate this to the world around them. If you were to ask most people in these churches, they would say this is completely untrue. It is one thing to say you believe in God based on a doctrine such as this and entirely another to let others see it in a way that is clear and evident to them.

Can we say that we are reaching the Lost in our communities? Statistics would say we are not. Gallop Reasearch Organization has said that forty percent of Americans attend church on Sunday and that these percentages have been pretty steady for years. According to the Harvard Institute of Religious Research, Americans tend to over exaggerate how often they attend. By actually counting the number of people who showed up at representative sample of churches, two researchers, Kirk Hadaway and Penny Marler found that only 20.4 percent of the population, or half the Gallup figure, attended church each weekend.

Palm Beach County, Florida, has a population of between 1.3 and 1.4 million. On any given Sunday morning in the United States, based on these statistics, about twenty percent of the people attend church. That means eighty percent do not attend any church and by every indication, do not intend to do so. Consequently. Palm Beach County has over a million people that do not attend church on any given Sunday.

If we assert that our doctrines are not simply dogma, wouldn't it be seen in our membership numbers increasing over time? If we reflect that first-century church, wouldn't it be evident by the Lord adding daily those who are being saved? I know you may feel the circumstances that lead to this situation are numerous and varied, but none of that makes any difference to the Lord. Man's plan and the enemy's devices cannot stand against God's Church.

Where is God in His Church? If He is there, they will know and will be drawn to Him, just as you and I were. When did our desire to have a church become the most important thing? Having a church is pointless if the church doesn't point others to Jesus.

How do we keep our doctrines from becoming dogma? We do so by focusing on His Mission and making it our own. When is the last time your church or fellowship thought about His Mission? I am not talking about your church's mission statement or vision statement. I am talking about seriously considering whether you were involved in Making Disciples. Do you spend time with Lost people, just getting to know them? Or is all your time spent with those in your fellowship?

Most of my exposure to the Lost comes through my business connections. I am blessed to own the companies I work for, and because of that, I have a platform where I am able to voice my beliefs in an environment I can control. I am also constantly under the watchful eyes of those with whom I share my faith. It keeps me honest, and hopefully it keeps me humble. If I am not consistent in my rhetoric, it is pointless to share my views at all.

What about you? Do you take the opportunity to share your faith with those with whom you come in contact? Would they know you are His followers by the way you live your life?

The denomination I belong to, as I have said, was birthed out of a call of God on a man who was a successful pastor. He pastored a large, wealthy church and was well compensated for his work there. But he knew the Mission was to reach the Lost, and he made that his priority. He answered the call, and a great missionary movement of God was born. Unfortunately, we cannot live on our past accomplishments. The world did not stop changing, and over time, this fellowship, which was reaching the world like few others had before, became a denomination. Although they did not stop reaching the world for Jesus, they did stop reaching their own communities for Him.

The results are evident and unfortunate. The unwillingness to see the need to move forward has become their undoing. This doctrine, along with the solid doctrinal statements of many other churches and denominations, did not change. However, the stagnation of their applications has created a dogma that must change.

Have we become the heretical religious elite that so incensed Jesus? Even if we can say we have not, is that what the world would say? If so, only we can change their viewpoint, and we can only do this by changing the way they see Jesus in us.

Style, not Substance

I attended my first elders' meeting in a church as the associate pastor in 2008. As we gathered in a small room at the church, one of the elders walked in and began to describe how a member of the church, who happened to be a relative, had to leave the service that morning because she became physically ill because of the drums. This person was in her eighties, and she could not sit and listen to that horrible sound. The words he used were, "That thump, thump, thump of the drums."

I sat there, completely astonished by what I was hearing. After a few minutes of listening to them talk about the musical styles and preferences, I asked them a simple question: "How many more decades do you think you will consider today's music contemporary?" They offered no response, and by doing so, basically dismissed my question. The real issue was one of style, not substance.

As the meeting progressed, it was brought to the attention of the board that two college-age sisters (there were very few people of that age group in this particular church) had left the church to go to one that was providing more of what they needed to grow spiritually. To my amazement, the comment was made, "Well, we can't be all things to all people."

From my perspective, this group of leaders, men who, if asked, would say they love the church and are committed to seeing it grow and reach the next generation for Christ, had just dismissed the future of their church to appease the past. I will not apologize for using the word "appease," because that is exactly what was happening, and that was the way they wanted it to be. If these young people couldn't find it in their hearts to see beyond what they wanted and consider what the church wanted, they could just go elsewhere.

These elders were irrelevant to these two young girls and, thereby, quite possibly to a culture, a culture that was all around them. They were also possibly irrelevant to some people sitting in their own church. They simply didn't understand why, or worse yet, didn't really care enough to want to know why.

This problem is not unique to this group of men or to this church. It is a systemic problem that is being used by the enemy to deepen the divide between generations. It is working amazingly well.

The idea that we cannot tolerate something other than what we want in the church is appalling. Are we not to reach the Lost for Jesus? Where do you suppose we will find them? How do you suppose we will reach them if we offer nothing to which they can relate? Can we do this without meeting them where they are? Is it our expectation that if they want to know Jesus, they need to come in line with what we believe is relevant?

Is this the example Jesus left us? Was he concerned about the way the established religious group of His day was doing church?

Or was He on a Mission and not willing to be deterred by the status quo? Hopefully, as you give thought to these questions, you will be humbled, as I have been, regarding your answers to them.

I heard someone say once, "If your issue is theology, stand firm. If it is personal preference, let it go." Do you suppose the issue concerning drums or the style of music was theological? Amazingly, some may argue it was. Or was the issue simply a matter of personal preference? Of course it was. Was it more important to have things the way they preferred, or was it more important to be able to reach the next generation for Jesus?

Were their hearts in the right place? I am sure if you were to ask them, they would say yes. I need to interject here that these were not bad men, intent on doing damage to the church or to the people in it. They were men who were blinded by what they saw as important. And to the detriment of everyone, they could not see anything else.

They were demonstrating a selfishness that is destructive and contributes to the death of a church. I know that Jesus said in Matthew 16:18 HCSB, "And I also say to you that you are Peter, and on this rock I will build My church, and the forces of Hades will not overpower it." and I definitely believe that is true. But it doesn't mean the Church in America will survive or that your church will survive. Does it? If you know anything at all about the state of the Church in America, you know churches are dying every day.

Many in the church I have mentioned have said that the communities' view of them it is not true. My comment is, and continues to be, that perception is reality. It is not necessarily the truth, but it is reality to those who believe it to be true.

Many will defend the negative comments about the church by reminding us that Christ said we would be persecuted.. 2 Timothy 3:12 HCSB reads, "In fact, all those who want to live a godly life in Christ Jesus will be persecuted." If we can say, as a church, that we are doing everything we can to love those around us, yes, we are living godly lives and will experience persecution. However, if we are building and maintaining barriers and creating hurdles that this next generation does not feel inclined to overcome, their perception is not unjustified, and we are not living godly lives.

Could we point to a particular person or group of people who are perpetuating this type of mind-set? As with any group or organization, we have to look at the leaders to find this answer. In my experience, organizations reflect the personality of their leaders. If these perceptions can be considered possible, we can say the reflection that is being given is not that of Jesus.

The Gatekeepers

Who are the gatekeepers?

They are the pastors, elders, and other church leaders. At least that is how it has been communicated to me by some in Church leadership. They consider themselves to be the "gatekeepers" of the Church.

I have always assumed they were referring to the passage in Matthew 7:13 HCSB, regarding entering the Kingdom of God: "Enter through the narrow gate. For the gate is wide and the road is broad that leads to destruction, and there are many who go through it." Or perhaps this is derived by considering verse 15 of that same chapter: "Beware of false prophets who come to you in sheep's clothing but inwardly are ravaging wolves."

I am sure the latter point regarding the keeping of the gate has to do with the shepherding aspect of pastoral ministry and the desire of these men to keep the wolves at bay. Are you guarding the gate or keeping the gate closed to protect the sheep, or to protect God? If it is the former, I think you should consider the way you are going about protecting them and from what you are protecting them. If it is the latter, that is a pretty lofty goal and one you and I most certainly cannot attain.

Before I can continue with this particular line of thought, I need everyone to understand my reasoning for what I say. First and foremost, it is not to be disparaging or to attack or cast dispersions on those in pastoral ministry or in Church leadership in general. As I have said, I have a license to do pastoral ministry myself, and I love to pray with and care for people and share God's Word with them when given the opportunity. As I have also said, my best friend is a pastor, and some of the finest men I know are pastors and leaders in churches and have spent their entire lives serving the Lord in ministry.

My primary reason for making this assertion is that there are some in church leadership today who have taken on the attitude of gatekeeper, and by doing so, are responsible for the perceptions of the Church that exist in the world today. It is our attitude that can cloud others' view of us. If we are not careful, it is this attitude that can cause us to overreach our responsibilities and cause others to see the worst in us.

Why do I suggest the gatekeepers may be responsible for our perception problem? The attitudes of those who are in charge tend to be reflected by those under them. The premise is one of gravity. Everything flows downhill.

When we present ourselves to the world around us as the guardians of our churches by being the gatekeepers, we become the very picture of what the world sees. I am afraid they are seeing a closed gate. This may not have been our intention, but it may be the result of our actions.

We must always be mindful of the way we are being perceived and consider the cost of closing our churches to our communities.

Many church leaders are committed to keeping their churches from the evils of the world. This is a noble cause but one that cannot be accomplished by any church leader. The only one who can keep our people from the evils of the world is Jesus, and He is not living behind the gate.

How do these gatekeepers hope to protect their people? I can only assume they hope to accomplish this by locking the gate and keeping out the world. The question I have is, are we keeping the evil of the world out and people in, or are we keeping people out and allowing evil to exist within?

We may be perpetuating one of the greatest evils: the evil of causing others to feel judged and unloved by the very ones who preach a message of grace and mercy.

How can we avoid this? Maybe if we open the gate wide enough and allow easy access to those who would come in and go out as they please, they will be able to see the beauty of knowing Jesus in an environment of fellowship that is Christ-centered and Spirit-led. We can certainly stand by the gate if we feel so compelled, but not as a guard, rather as a host, welcoming all with open arms.

I have already told you of Ravi Zacharias' assertion from his book and Video series, <u>Deliver Us from Evil</u>, copyright 1996 by Word publishing. In the 50's and 60's the Church closed its doors to the world and lost their social significance. In light of this, perhaps it is time for us to open the gate and trust the Lord for our protection, instead of trying to protect Him and His people ourselves.

The passage said the gate is narrow, it did not say it was closed.

When we have this perspective, we must be careful that we don't lose sight of what God says is important and don't become consumed by what we think is important. The idea that believers of a God who made it His Mission to send His Son into this world to save what was lost now wants people He calls to keep this same lost world out of His church is an astonishingly sad revelation.

We must be careful how we see ourselves as it relates to God's plan for the salvation of mankind. We are His instruments for His use. We are not Him, and He and His Church are not solely for our use.

A CALL TO WORSHIP

In 2004, as I was driving home with my wife and son from visiting our daughter at college, I was overwhelmed with a sense of knowing the Church needed to demonstrate unity to the world. I truly believe this had to be the Lord, because it is not every day that I sit around contemplating the lack of unity that may or may not exist in the Church. If you know me, you know this is true. You also know that I can be as self-absorbed as the next guy, and I want to deflect any visions of grandeur away from me and unto Him.

I just kept thinking how awesome it would be if we could have all the churches in Palm Beach County, where I live, come together for a day of corporate worship. In my mind, there would be no big-name speakers, and no single church would spearhead the event. It would be comprised of speakers from all different denominations and ethnic groups, and Jesus would be the focus. The emphasis would be we are all united in Christ. We are all the Body of Christ.

Sounds simple enough doesn't it? At least, that was what I thought.

Well, I started with my own pastor. I called him as I drove home and shared what I had been considering. I will call it a vision. He said, "That sounds great John, but they will never go for it. There are too many differences, and besides, they won't even come together to fellowship with each other as pastors, let alone involve their churches."

Being my usual self, I said, "Well, that's okay. We may not be able to get them to do it, but God can."

I need to say he became one of the truest believers in what we were trying to accomplish and, as with every aspect of my relationship with him, one of my staunchest supporters. From then on, he helped me make inroads into local ministeriums and set up a meeting with one that met in the western communities of Palm Beach County.

He got me together with a group of pastors that met on a fairly regular basis. I shared with them what the Lord had laid on my heart. They were attentive and not discouraging, but I think it is safe to say they were skeptical, telling me in essence that if this were something the Lord was telling me to do, by all means I should do it. However, they were unwilling to help, except for a Pastor named Calvin Lyerla of Acts 2, an Assembly of God church in Loxahatchee, FL. Calvin caught the vision right away and would go on to become instrumental in helping us to bring this together. This was a burden he shared. In fact, it was Calvin who was the driving force behind their monthly meetings. He believed in the need for the Body to support one another, and he supported me and the group every step of the way.

We began our effort to gather believers from across denominational lines to have a single day of corporate worship for the sole purpose of demonstrating unity to our community.

A Call to Worship was what we called this event, and those involved were selfless in their efforts and support. For that, I am eternally grateful.

After meeting with these men, the next step was to contact other churches in our community. I tried to contact pastors in my community. I began with the largest church in our area. I shared this vision and asked if they would be interested in being a part of this event. Although I was not able to speak with their pastor, his secretary told me they would not be able to participate, because they had their own things going on. It was a disappointment, but as my pastor had told me, "They would never go for it"—they being the pastors of the established churches in our area.

I would like to point out that although this particular church would not be able and did not participate in the event, they did, however, let us have a meeting at their facility to promote the event. It was well attended. I am thankful for their allowing us to do that.

I ended up with six pastors from six churches, representing three different denominations and one para-church organization, as our steering committee. They were David Lane (CMA), Calvin Lyerla (Assemblies of God), Carlton Gant (PLF), (Dale Locke (UMC), Brian Shore (CMA), Teddy O'Farrell (CMA), and Bill Hochstetler (YFC of Palm Beach County). My wife, Bonnie, joined the board a little later. I will be forever grateful to these men for their willingness to consider it a possibility in the face of pretty heavy odds.

They were all amazing and spent countless hours praying and meeting to help pull off something that had never been done in our area and has not been done since. I was blessed, and still am, by their faithfulness and willingness to be involved.

We also had businesspeople who contributed. They were Alan Gerwig (Alan Gerwig and Associates), Dale Hedrick (Hedrick Brothers Construction), and our company (J. W. Fire Sprinkler, Inc.). We could not have done any of it without these people. Because of their contributions, the entire event was paid for, to the tune of $26,000.

I would also like to give a tremendous thanks to my best friend and the love of my life, Bonnie, who gave of herself during this period, as did my children, Lindsay and John. I love you all from the bottom of my heart. The enemy was very active in the personal lives of my family during the planning and organizing that was required, and though my family experienced some serious adversity, they also never wavered. It is their love and support of me that kept me focused and grounded during this period.

It was at this point that I began to meet with businesspeople and pastors from across our county. Bill, with YFC, was instrumental in helping me meet most of them. He introduced me to one businessman in particular who helped Luis Palau' do a huge event in Ft. Lauderdale the previous year. I am sorry I do not remember his name.

He listened to me intently and then told me it sounded good, but if we were going to get people interested, if we were going to be successful, we needed a hook.

My answer to this assertion was very matter of fact and said with the utmost confidence, "We have a hook. It is Jesus."

He kind of halfheartedly said, "Okay."

One of the men present at the initial meeting with the western community pastors wanted to know from my pastor how effective I was in witnessing for Jesus. His concern was that before I could tell others about the need to be unified, I needed to demonstrate a life that pointed others to Jesus. I assume my pastor told him I did. I can only say my impression of his question was to protect the Church from someone who wasn't practicing what he was preaching.

The guard was on duty, and the gate was secure!

It was also brought to my attention by one of the pastors on our committee that the head of the denomination he belonged to in our area wanted to know if this event should be coming from a layman, which I was at the time. He thought it should be coming from someone in the clergy. The gatekeeper is ever vigilant!

On another occasion, when I was meeting with the pastor of a large mainstream church in our area to ask him to be a part of what we believed the Lord was trying to do here, he told me, "I am careful whom I fellowship with." I was taken aback by this statement, and to this day, I am sure this type of attitude plays a big part in the perceptions the world has of the Church. The gate is officially closed!

My first consideration was to respond to Him with, "Well, thankfully Jesus wasn't." If He was careful whom He fellowshipped with, I wouldn't be here. Fortunately for me, I didn't say that. I just continued with what I felt the Lord would have me say, and we parted amicably. By the way, his church did not participate and did not fellowship with us on the day of the event.

Fortunately for me, during this period, no matter what was said, I was able to respond in an appropriate manner. Or so I have been told. If that is the case, and those who know me know if it is true, the Lord had to be in it, because I have never been known for my diplomacy.

There was a lot of momentum leading up to this event. Then, the day it was to happen, a hurricane hit our area, and the event had to be postponed for a year. It did end up happening about a year later, but it seemed to have lost all the momentum that had been created prior to the storm.

We ended up with between eight hundred and nine hundred people in attendance. Not the number we had hoped for, but we all believe the ones who came were the ones the Lord wanted to be there.

I have to add a final thought which points to the gatekeeping that I had referred to earlier. Even though there was no money asked for during the planning and scheduling and no offering was taken, along with the fact that it was attended by many pastors who did not bring their churches, I can only assume this points to the fact they were making sure this was what we had claimed it to be before they would promote it to their congregations.

They were guarding the gate, and in doing so, they may very well have missed a Holy Spirit moment that was there for the taking. I guess only the Lord knows the answer to that. The one thing I know is that my life is better because of all those who took the risk of involving themselves in the Call to Worship.

Thank you all, and God bless you!

This event and the participation, and the lack thereof, has led many to ask questions regarding the Church in our area. What is it that makes us so skeptical of one another? Why did so many choose not to be involved? How do we suppose this is seen by the world? How do we overcome the things that prevent us from involving ourselves with one another? I do not have the answers to these questions, but I do know that what was needed in this case was a willingness to look outside our own church walls to see a bigger picture of the Church and its purposes in our world, and a willingness to see God at work among His people and His people at work among the Lost.

The churches in our area just needed to trust the Lord enough to open the gate. How many other moments do you think we might have missed under the guise of protecting God and His people? I am thankful I was able to learn from this experience, and I hope to practice in further service to Him.

Restoring Honor

On August 28, 2010, there was an event in Washington, DC called Restoring Honor, which. in essence, was about calling all Americans to return to their Judeo-Christian roots. The purpose, as I understood it, was to return our nation to God.

Bonnie and I attended this event and can attest to the fact that from the opening prayer, to those honored for their contributions to our country, to the closing prayer and the singing of "Amazing Grace," Jesus Christ was high and lifted up. I was blessed to have been there and am truly hoping that perhaps this is a true movement of God.

This event was met by many Christians with the same skepticism and concern we had experienced during the planning and organizing of the Call to Worship event in 2005. The main difference, besides the fact that it was on a much grander scale, was that it was an appeal to the nation to turn back to God. Ours was an appeal to the Church in our community to demonstrate the unity of the Church.

Glenn Beck, a radio and television personality, was the man who organized this event. Many Christians share the view that Mr. Beck, because he is a Mormon, should not or cannot lead a movement for God, making this event meaningless, even heretical, as far as the kingdom is concerned. My question is, if God can use men like Pharaoh, Nebuchadnezzar, and Saul of Tarsus to further His kingdom and bring glory to Himself, can He not use Glenn Beck, a Mormon, or any other man to do the same? I believe He not only can but will, if He should choose to do so.

God—not you or I—chooses whom he uses, and I thank Him for that. Not only can He do this, but He does so on a regular basis. We are not charged with protecting God. We have been charged with bearing witness of Jesus in hopes of reaching the Lost. Can we do that if we are constantly fighting among ourselves, distrusting one another, and then shouting it from the rooftops for the world to hear?

Is this what Jesus would be communicating?

As with denominational issues previously discussed, is it about doctrine, or is it just dogma? Whom are we protecting? Is it Jesus, or is it the way we want to see things done?

Are we willing to see things through a different lens, the lens of grace, or will we continue to see the world through rose-colored glasses? I pray that I will take each of these questions and give them prayerful consideration. I hope you will do the same.

I believe the time has come to shift our thinking to a new paradigm. We need to do that by going back to the beginning of the Church, where faith and belief in Jesus were the focus, and where God began to build His Church. We must begin to reestablish Christ's Church.

Re-establishing
Christ's Church

What must we do to overcome the issues that are causing the world to view us with disdain?

Where do we begin? We must begin by looking inside the Church and inside our own hearts. We—I— must start by removing the blinders that don't allow me to see my own faults. I don't think I am alone when I say it is a lot easier for me to see the fault in someone else than it is to see the fault in me.

If we don't start with ourselves, we will miss the problem all together. Do you hear what I am telling you? You and I may very well be the problem. It is doubtful that we are the entire problem, but we certainly may be adding to it.

We must ask ourselves, as with the question on humility, if we are feeding the perceptions the world has of the Church. Are we a part of the problem? If so, the sooner we can identify that, the sooner we can start to correct it.

If all the things I have written about from my limited experiences can be considered as representative of what is happening in the Church today, we have a problem. I believe that problem is we have an identity crisis. When the world looks at us, they do not see in us what we see in ourselves. They do not identify us as something worth their while.

We are seen by the world as divided. We have become unrecognizable, or perhaps we are being recognized for what we have become. To reestablish the Church is to take us back to the attitude we see in that first Church in the book of Acts, the one that was seen by its world as so attractive, Act 2:47 HCSB, "And every day the Lord added to them those who were being saved".

The problem we face today in America is that Christ's Church has lost its focus. To correct this problem, we will have to begin with refocusing ourselves on Him and His Mission, and take the focus off ourselves and our mission.

Clearly, if you can identify with any of the things I have discussed up to now, you have to admit we have lost our focus on what is important and, to quote a song by Seven Mary Three, have become cumbersome to this world. Cumbersome means difficult to handle, troublesome, or onerous.

Can you understand from where this perception may come? Is there any justification for it? If you have ever sat on a church board, you know this is very true. I am certain this is not how we want to be perceived. However, we must be able to recognize and agree that this may be the way we are being seen, and it is indicated by our lack of social significance.

Is my assertion incorrect? Was Ravi Zacharias wrong? Are we socially insignificant?

If the statistics I gave earlier—about the 80 percent of the people who don't attend church on any given Sunday—is the evidence then, I think there can be no doubt. If we were socially significant, relevant to our culture and communities, more people would be coming to church on Sunday morning. People are most definitely involved in things they see as significant. But if we are seen as cumbersome, it makes sense that they are staying home.

Where have we gone wrong? I believe the problem may be that we have reverted to a religion and lost the relationship Jesus died to establish. Our focus as a Church has become internal instead of external. We have become all about us, while He was all about them.

We have once again become so heavenly minded that we are of no earthly good. We have become a Church focused on ministry and not a Church focused on the Mission.

Can we say this is true of the Church? What about us as individuals? Have we become focused on the external instead of internal, has our passion for Jesus Christ become lost in our pursuit of a religion we have created for our own purposes and, yes, for our own pleasures?

If we are honest, we can see that the problem is we have moved ahead of God, and consequently, we have lost our way. The beauty of our situation, because of His grace and mercy, is that it is never too late for us to change direction. It is never too late for us to repent and refocus ourselves on Him. He is, as He has always been, waiting for us to turn to Him.

Do we see the need to do that? Is it possible that the Mission of the Church has lost its significance to the Church? Has reaching the Lost been replaced with being lost? Has loving others and loving Him been replaced with loving ourselves and protecting Him?

Does the possibility of even a few of the things I have tried to point out matter enough for us to consider them as an area where improvement may be needed? You and I are to carry His Gospel to the ends of the earth, and that starts here at home. Unfortunately, we may have forgotten His purpose and become overwhelmed with our own. Can this be a reason for some of the perception problems that exist?

If the way we are viewed detracts from His Mission, we have to change the way we are seen; we have to change the perspective others have of us. We cannot do that by telling them they are wrong. We can only do it by showing them they are wrong. We can only do that if we can show them something they want to see.

The Mission of the Church is paramount and cannot be overstated. The battle is still raging all around us. The enemy remains undeterred, and he is winning in his effort to create an ineffective version of the Church. I make no apologies for stating the obvious. The numbers of those not in attendance on any given Sunday morning speak for themselves.

What is really sad is the fact that you and I, as believers, are safe. Our salvation is assured. However, those we have been charged with reaching are floundering in the darkness, convinced it is not worth being a part of what they see in us. They are not being drawn to Him, because they are repelled by us. Therefore, they flirt with an eternity separated from God, and we are watching them from our sanctuaries as they do.

There are many reasons people are willing to take such a risk. This forces me to ask myself, does it matter to me? I would also like you to consider whether it matters to you. If we can answer yes, we must ask ourselves, what can we do about it? How can we help to change their perceptions of the Church?

We have to begin with the understanding that change is needed and warranted. Hopefully, I have been able to at least get you to consider this as a possibility. If we are going to reestablish Christ's Church, it has to start with an agreement that there is a need to do so. We must also agree that He can use someone we may see as unqualified or even ill-equipped to bring forth His message.

If we can determine that a perception problem regarding the Church exists in our world today, perhaps we can begin to look for solutions to bring about a reestablishing of the Church in our world.

The new paradigm has to be a return to the old paradigm. It has to start with Jesus, His Words, and His Mission. It has to be led by the Holy Spirit, and it has to be intentional in its pursuit of living lives that point others to him.

This is where we begin.

Focused Vision

We have to refocus on Jesus. As with everything in our lives, it has to start with Him, with prayer, with the reading and studying of His Word, and with living a life that reflects Him and our belief in Him. Our lives must bear witness to what it is we believe.

We should begin with a right perspective of who God is. Our perspective should not begin with the music, the state of the Church or the world today—whether it is worse off today than it has ever been—or whether things are being done the way we think they should be.

Instead, we must start by simply placing God in His rightful place in our lives. Before we can answer the question, where is God in His Church, we must be able to answer the question, where is He in our lives? Is He the Lord of our lives, really the Lord of our lives? Does He rule in our lives? Do we see Him clearly? Do we see Him at all?

Our focus has to begin with a right view of Him and where we have placed Him in our lives. In order to see where we go from here, our vision has to begin by focusing on Him. This focused vision begins when we have an understanding of who God is and of what He is revealing to us. When we understand what our Mission is and for what He is calling us, we can learn to focus on that Mission in our churches, in our ministries, and in our lives. This is not anything new.

The question is, are we applying it to our lives? Rick Warren's book The Purpose-Driven Life published by Zondervan, in 2002,

I am told, exemplifies this by starting with a simple statement: "It is not about you." Our vision of God has to begin with this simple yet profound truth. The Mission we have undertaken as disciples of Jesus Christ is not about us. It is about Him!

If it is about Him, they—the Lost—will see this and be drawn to Him. Is this the case in your churches and fellowships? Are people being drawn to Jesus because of what they see in you? If 80 percent are not attending a church on Sunday, no matter how good you may feel about what you are involved in, you have to admit that the Church, the Body, is not being seen this way, and you and I are a part of that Body.

He has to be the reason we gather together on Sundays, or whatever day of the week we may gather, because He is the source of our salvation and redemption. It is to Him that we bow down and pray. Anyone you ask who has been a believer for any length of time will most likely agree with these statements and would most likely say their lives reflect these things.

But the world we are all a part of does not share this view. Do you think this is their fault or ours?

In almost every book I've read and almost every person with whom I have spoken, one thing remains consistent. Our ability to see clearly begins with seeking God and His purpose, not with seeking ourselves or with trying to fulfill our own purposes.

When we lose our focus on Jesus, our vision becomes clouded, and we are unable to see what we need to do and where we need to go.

How do we begin to develop this focused vision? We begin by returning to the old paradigm. We must begin by making Jesus our focus. Is this possible? In this world of nonstop information and instant access to it, can we truly focus on anything? I ask these kinds of questions because I am not sure myself. I am the quintessential multitasker. If I am not thinking or working on several things at once, I am underwhelmed and distracted.

Can I really have focus? What does it mean to have focus? To have focus means to have a point of concentration, something on which to direct our attention. We must have a point of emphasis. God has to become our point of emphasis, and this happens when our intellect, our heart, and our will focus their energies reverently and affectionately upon Him. Doesn't that make sense? Is He your point of emphasis? If so, the result will be love: passionate, ever-present, ever-dominant love. Love first for Him and then love for others. It is this kind of love that can change the perceptions of a world that has long since grown weary of what they have seen in the Church.

Can we make Him our point of emphasis? I am convinced that we cannot unless we start by intentionally involving ourselves in carrying out His Mission. To have a focused vision, we need to have the ability to concentrate on, pay attention to, and give emphasis to the direction we need to go as an individual, as a people, and as a church. We also need to do so with our intellect, heart, and will.

Jesus spoke clearly on the subject in His Sermon on the Mount in Matthew 5. This sermon is meant to give us a focused vision on life. As you know, it is divided into five sections:

Beatitudes—Teachings that begin with "Blessed." These were meant to comfort suffering believers.

New Laws—Contrasts the old Law of Moses with the new law of Christ, a brief summary of Christian doctrine.

Lord's Prayer—Instructions on prayer. Jesus also teaches the proper motives for fasting and offering gifts.

Money—Christian attitudes concerning the use of money. Reasons to avoid worry.

Warnings—Dangers of false teachers and hypocrisy. Jesus also presents the parable of the wise and foolish builders.

Based on the premises we have been discussing, this seems to me to be the perfect place to begin to discover how we can refocus ourselves, as a body of believers, on Jesus and His Mission.

In this passage of Scripture, Jesus is telling us how we can be blessed if we are willing to see the world with a focus on God. In every case, we see a condition of the heart that requires a focused vision of God in our lives, don't we? We see brokenness, mourning, and meekness represented here. We see a desire to please God and the need to show mercy. We need to have a heart that seeks God first, not one that seeks our own desires or self-interests.

Each of the points Christ makes in this passage point to placing God first in our lives. After we have done that, we are given a picture of the results of our willingness to do so.

Start with a Pure Heart

From where does this focused vision come? What is Jesus telling us? Isn't He is telling us that we have to begin by having a pure heart—a heart that seeks to please Him and to reach those who don't know Him?

What does it mean to you to be pure in heart? Does it mean to obey God's law and live right lives? To have a heart that is focused on doing good? Certainly, these are fine things and would be a by-product of a pure heart. But I believe there is a deeper meaning to what Jesus teaches us here. To have a heart so pure that we will see God, we must have a single-minded focus on God.

Throughout God's Word, we see examples of men and women of God who have been clearly focused on God and then, for different reasons, they lost their focus, and the results were unfortunate.

Adam and Eve, who walked with God in the Garden, clearly had vision and focus. They could see the beauty of God's creation. You would think walking with God would give you a vision and focus that could sustain, wouldn't you? And yet, they lost focus. Their inability to maintain their focus on God is the reason we experience sin and death today. The consequences of their loss of focus have had eternal consequences for all of mankind.

We see Abraham, a man found righteous by God. God spoke to him and promised to birth a nation and bless a people through him.

You would think talking with God would give you vision that you could sustain, wouldn't you? Yet Abraham and his wife, Sara, lost focus. They could not wait on God's promise of a son and moved ahead of God. The results were the birth of Ishmael through Hagar, and the consequences are still felt throughout our world today.

There are many other examples throughout God's Word. We could look at the people of Israel as a whole, who constantly had vision of God's presence in their lives, and yet they would lose focus and forget what God had done for them and the promises He had made to them. We can look at David, Solomon, and the many kings after them. Each of them had a vision of God's will for their lives, yet they lost focus because of their own desires and agendas, and the results in every case were destructive.

One of the greatest examples of seeing a vision of God and losing focus is Peter, in Matthew 16:16 HCSB, where Peter says, "You are the Messiah, the Son of the living God!" Shortly thereafter, we see Peter deny Him three times. His vision had become clouded by fear and self-preservation, and the results were Peter lost his focus on the Lord.

Are you and I any different from these men and women of God? Are we any less capable of having a vision from God in our lives and our church? Are we any less capable of losing focus and relying on our own efforts and abilities, instead of allowing Him to work in and through us?

My hope is that we can commit together to develop a Pure Heart that will allow us to see God. Can we do that? Can we make it a goal at church and in our personal lives to seek after God in all we do? Will you ask God to help you have a single-minded focus on Him? I know it is a tall order in a world that constantly distracts us, but if we will do this, I am convinced others will see in us what they saw in that first church, and their perception of God and His Church will be one they want to be a part of, not one that repels them.

Serving God

As our focus becomes clearer and we begin to make God our point of emphasis, the by-product will become service to Him and to others. We will be compelled to serve Him. This compulsion is no trivial matter.

Our service to God and service to one another are the very foundations on which God has established His Church. Jesus' death on the Cross was an act and example of service. He was serving His Father by being obedient to His will, and He was serving us by providing a way for us to be reconciled to God. His act of service was one of obedience and was motivated by love for His Father and for us.

Likewise, our service to Him must be motivated by this same kind of love. We should desire to serve Him out of our gratitude to Him for the way He demonstrated His love for us. We have been commanded to serve Him by loving Him and others, and we have been shown the example of service through His life, death, and resurrection. We need to demonstrate our love for Him to others through our desire to serve Him. We need to see our service as an opportunity to demonstrate that gratitude to God for what He has done for us and is doing in our lives.

We should want to serve Him and others, because we love Him and others. As with His service to us, our service to Him should be motivated by this love. When we accept Jesus as our Lord and Savior, we are given the command in Matthew 22:36–40, to serve Him by loving the Lord and loving one another. It is also something we should desire to do in our hearts.

We have the privilege of being able to serve Him with our time, talents, and treasures. Giving and serving are acts of love. These are the things that draw people to Jesus and to His Church. Music, preaching, or even the building may get them to come to church, but it is the presence of the love of Christ and the love for each other that keeps them coming back. Why are you serving or attending your church? In almost every case, you are drawn there by love.

As we continue to consider the results of reestablishing a Christ-centered Church, I would like for us to consider that when we serve Him, we serve Him as His Ambassadors.

Have you ever thought of yourself in that regard? An Ambassador is a representative. You and I are representatives for Christ. As with witnessing, we are representatives wherever we go and whatever we do. This is our greatest act of service, and it is carried out in many ways. We can certainly go to the ends of the earth as a missionary and witness for Jesus. We also must understand that we give witness to Him in every aspect of our lives. Remember the clothesline?

Not only have we been commanded to serve Him by loving Him and others, we have also been commissioned to serve Him as His Ambassadors. In Matthew 28:18–20, we are told, "Go into the world and make disciples," to tell the Good News to the world, letting them know that He is the way to salvation.

Jesus says in Acts 1:8 HCSB, "but you will receive power when the Holy Spirit comes on you; and you will be my witnesses in Jerusalem, and in all Judea and Samaria, and to the ends of the earth." Are you empowered by this reality, or are you intimidated by it? If you are like me, it is probably a little of both. One thing for sure is this truth gives evidence to the contention that the view the world has of the Church today is brought on by the Church today. The Church is what they see in you and me.

There is no doubt that we can damage the Church, and ultimately Jesus, with our witness, but we also have the tremendous opportunity to serve Him by our witness. When we accept Him as our Lord and Savior, our next act of service is to be a witness for Him, to represent Him to our world. We serve Him by showing Him to others through the way we live our lives, and we share Him with those we come in contact with when we live lives that point to Him.

Have you ever considered that your life and the way you live it is an act of service to God? Being Christ's Ambassadors, living our lives well before others, is perhaps our most important act of service. We make disciples by leading them to Christ and allowing them to see Him at work in our lives. But we must remember that this requires us to live our lives well by God's standards, not by our own standards. When we can do this, others will see Him in us and be drawn to Him because of what they see.

To seek to serve Jesus in our lives and in our church is to understand that we need to do so by serving Him and others. As with everything that Jesus did, we use His example of service and give of ourselves. It is not out of some desire to have a position, or of some sense of superiority; it is out of a heart that seeks to serve.

Service to God gives us a chance to give back. We need to do so, as with being able to see God by having a pure heart. You and I should serve God because it is the desire of our hearts. We should be obedient to Him and His commission and command, understanding that it is not going to lift us up, but will lift Him up. Service to God is an act of placing Him and others first. We serve Him in our homes, workplaces, and churches. We serve Him wherever He has placed us.

We serve Him as friends and neighbors, as sons and daughters, as husbands and wives, and as fathers and mothers. We serve Him by giving of our time, talents, and treasures. We serve Him by caring for one another, sharing with one another, and by worshipping Him together.

It is through these simple selfless acts of service that God will use us to continue to establish His Church by changing the hearts of men and women both inside and outside the Church.

When our hearts and minds are focused on Jesus, we can see each day as another chance to serve Him by allowing Him to use us in the sphere of influence in which He has placed us. We do not have to seek a position with God, because He has already chosen where we should serve. The question becomes, will you?

If loving God and each other, if being a witness for Jesus is what we are doing wherever we go, and if serving Him and each other leads others to Christ, what keeps us from accomplishing that? Is it a fear of being inadequate or ridiculed? We have all probably felt these things at one point or another. Perhaps we feel overwhelmed by the responsibility of being His witness to others. I am sure in my life, at different points, it may have been a little of either of these things.

The one thing I know is that God will equip us to serve where He desires us to serve. My life gives testimony to this, as can be confirmed by those who have known me for any period of time.

ORDINARY PEOPLE FOR HIS EXTRAORDINARY CALLING

Who can serve Him? Anyone He chooses!

I am proof that if the Lord can use someone like me, He can use anyone. His Word gives us evidence of this, time and time again. God has always used ordinary people for his extraordinary calling."

We see this clearly in the book of 1 Corinthians. Paul, in his greeting to the church at Corinth, reminds them of their calling to be Holy (to be saintly; godly; pious; devout) and of the fact they have been sanctified (set apart), along with all those that believe in Jesus. Through their belief in Christ, they have been, as stated in 1 Corinthians 1:5 HCSB "made rich in everything—in all speaking and all knowledge," which is being seen in their lives and gives witness to Paul's testimony about Jesus.

Based solely on Paul's words about the Corinthian church, would you say the perceptions their world had of them are the same as the ones we have been discussing regarding the Church in America today? I don't think so. He said their belief in Jesus, which was being seen in their lives, was giving witness to his testimony about Christ. Can that be said about me, or you? If not, why not? You and I, when we accept Jesus as Lord, have this same calling, to be holy. We are to live lives that point to Jesus. I would like to reiterate here that we are set apart from, not removed, from the world. We cannot possibly affect the world if we are not in the world, can we?

The Church at Corinth was filled with ordinary people just like you and me, and their lives and the way they were living them, even in the way they were speaking, pointed others to Jesus. Can that be said of us? If it could, wouldn't our churches be growing? Wouldn't the Lord be adding to our numbers daily those who are being saved? This is really the crux of this entire book.

Where is God in His Church? He is where we have placed Him. Can those around us see what Paul was saying about the Corinthian church? If not, why not? Are we no more capable of being used by God than they were? If our focus is on Him and our service is to bring Him glory, we will be seen just as they were. Until that transpires, we will not. No matter how much we claim we are not how we are being portrayed by the world, we cannot change what they claim to see until we show them something different.

Paul states in 1 Corinthians chapter 12 that because of their faith and the way they are living, they are not lacking in any spiritual gift. This allows them to remain strong to the end and blameless when Christ returns. He tells us here in 1 Corinthians 1:4-11, that these spiritual gifts, which they received because of their faith, were manifestations of the Holy Spirit. They included wisdom, knowledge, faith, healing, miraculous powers, prophecy, the ability to distinguish between spirits, and the ability to speak in and interpret tongues. These gifts were given by the Holy Spirit when He determined they were needed.

Just by knowing this, can't you see how we can overcome our fear of change and our tendencies to be intimidated by our need to serve Him and others?

What makes these people any different than you and me? We are children of the same God. We have been left with the same Spirit to guide us, to teach us, to rebuke us, to empower us, and to equip us for service.

I am not sure if this is what makes them different or not. I certainly hope not. But what they were demonstrating to their world and what was seen and identified by Paul was "faith." Their faith was strong enough to overcome their fears and shortcomings. Why? Because they knew, as we should know, that when God calls His people to serve Him, He does not leave them empty-handed. He equips them with everything they need to carry out the Mission to which He has called them.

What do you say we step out in faith and do what we have been called to do!

In the next part of this chapter from 1 Corinthians, Paul goes on to reinforce the importance of unity and the need to be in full agreement in mind and thought. This particular group of people was being divided into camps, which was creating division and emptying the truth of the Cross of its power.

Would you say we are unified as a Church? The perception problems we have been discussing this entire time are based on the reality that the world sees the Church as one entity. We may not identify with those churches that are involved in some of the awful things we read about or watch on the news, but that is who we are to the world.

Isn't it interesting that we don't see ourselves this way? We may see our denominations as one, or maybe we will even stretch out and include evangelicals as one. If we are honest, aren't we careful with whom we fellowship?

If we can agree there is not a unified front in the Church of Jesus Christ today among those of us who call ourselves Christians, how do you suppose this looks to the world? Do you suppose they see division in the Church as a house divided? Jesus told us that house could not stand. Isn't it a reasonable assumption that this is how the world views the Church? Even if you do not agree with any of my assertions about the causes of these perceptions, you do not have to look very far to find something in your own sphere of influence that gives credibility to their claims. If so, we need to understand

and to admit that division causes angst and disharmony within the Church. And it creates confusion and doubt among those outside the Church.

Division affects the world's perception of the Church.

Could this be where their viewpoint originates? How can we overcome this? Is it too late for the Church in America? Many would say so. However, I am not convinced this is the case. I believe there are still too many who have not heard the Gospel for God to remove us from His Mission. My hope and prayer for my community is that we can show them a Church that worships a God who still draws men to Himself.

So how do we do this? Well, let me go back to the point of God using ordinary people for his extraordinary calling. How many of us see ourselves as being wise by human standards? Are any of us influential? Or how many are of noble birth? If you answered no or none to any of these questions, that is exactly why you can be used and exactly why you have been called. You are exactly the kind of person God is looking for and exactly the kind of person He uses.

God has not stopped calling people unto Himself. Do you know that you have been called to salvation through Jesus? Though you and I chose to accept Him, it is He who called us, and now He is calling us to serve Him.

How do we know He uses people like us? Paul gives us the answer in 1 Corinthians 1:28 HCSB: "God has chosen the world's insignificant and despised things—the things viewed as nothing—so He might bring to nothing the things that are viewed as something."

Christians of the day were seen as lowly and despised by their contemporaries. Is it any different today? Consider what is being said about the Church in America today. The whole premise of this book, regarding perception being reality, hinges on the point that we are seen as lowly and without value, social significance or influence. Worse yet, we are seen as hypocritical, judgmental, and with a sense of superiority.

Fortunately, there is hope for us yet. He has always used the undervalued, the insecure, and the overlooked to do His will. Throughout His Word, common men and women have been used for uncommon purposes. These include Abraham, Moses, David, and the like. Men like Paul, Peter, James, John, and the twelve, and women like Rachel, Ruth, and Mary were all used by God for purposes far beyond the appearance of their status or abilities, far beyond what they thought they were capable of.

Why not you and me? Are we not called to serve Him? Are we not capable of being used in His service? Why does He do this? In verses 29–31 of this same chapter in Corinthians, Paul tells us God does this, "so that no one can boast in His presence. It is because of Him that you are in Christ Jesus, who has become for us wisdom from God—that is, our righteousness, holiness and redemption." That is the reason you and I can serve Him and allow others to see Him in our lives.

God is still in the business today of using ordinary people for His extraordinary calling. The importance of this calling cannot be underestimated. The privilege of this calling cannot be overemphasized. The purpose of this calling cannot be overlooked. God calls all mankind to His saving grace through Christ Jesus. Unfortunately, not everyone answers that call.

Do you believe that God can use you? Is He calling you to know Jesus for the first time? Is He calling you to know Him more? If so, will you answer that call? Is He calling you to service? Are you answering that call?

If He can use shepherds, prostitutes, fishermen, and persecutors of His Church to change the world and confound the wise, what makes you think He can't use someone like you or me?

The question is will we answer His call?

Where Do We Go from Here?

I am sure by now I have ruffled many feathers and perhaps even caused some of you to reach a point of anger. As I have said, it was never my intention to do that. If what I have said has offended you, I am truly sorry. But if what the Lord has said offends you, I make no apologies for that.

The point of all this has been to try and establish a point of reference for the perception of reality that many in our world have regarding the Church specifically and Christians in general. I believe I have done that by giving some examples of my personal experiences in ministry and by asking each person reading this to consider his own experiences and perhaps even personal feelings and viewpoints regarding these impressions.

I also have asked enough questions that we should have been able to determine whether we are able to see our way clear to consider if these experiences point to a systemic problem within the Church today, and if so, what the possibilities for dealing with those problems may be.

I believe the evidence is before us. And unfortunately, to those in our world, our communities, and to some degree in our churches, these views may appear insurmountable. Fortunately for those of us who know Jesus, we know that nothing is insurmountable with God. No matter how many times we may stumble, no matter how many times we may head off in the wrong direction, it is never too late to turn our eyes to Jesus and find our way back to where He would have us go.

This is really the only choice we have as a Church. We cannot deny that these perceptions exist, even if we disagree with them. Our best way forward is to accept that these beliefs exist and to care enough to see the need to address them as legitimate concerns.

If a perception of the Church as being judgmental, hypocritical, and having a sense of superiority cannot be an acceptable way for us to be seen. Then I think you can agree we must do everything we can to deal with these views directly and with a sense of purpose. Life is fragile, and our time is fleeting. Jesus could return at any moment, and those of us who know Him have nothing to worry about. But all around us are people who do not know Him. They are Lost and have this unfortunate perspective of His Church.

Therefore, one thing is certain. We must see the need to address these issues before it is too late. We have so little time, and we have so much work to do.

Where do we go from here? We go back to the point I have been raising. We go back to asking ourselves, "Where is God in His Church?"

WHERE IS GOD IN HIS CHURCH?

My hope in writing this is as much for me as it is for anyone who might read it. I feel very strongly about the importance of the perceptions of our world as it watches God's Church. I am convinced that we are still responsible for carrying out His Mission and for growing His Church. I am also convinced I have fallen short in my effort to do this and truly believe that I am not alone.

I hope I have given us some food for thought regarding our own lives and the roles we may be playing in fostering the perceptions that exist. My hope is to bring about a positive change within my own life and in the lives of those with whom I come in contact.

I have told you of the loss of both of my parents over the last five years and the impact that has had on my life. The one positive thing that has occurred regarding those loses is that I have gained a true sense of urgency about the *Mission and the Message* of Jesus Christ.

Since the suicide of one of my best friends, Don McKinney, and the deaths of my mom and dad, my personal goal has been to let everyone I know and love know about Jesus. Throughout this writing, and to the glory of God, my eyes have been opened to the realization that this includes everyone, not just those I know and love.

I am also keenly aware that I will not be able to do this if I am considered a representative of a Church that is giving the world a bad impression of what a Christian is, or worse, of who Jesus is. I want to be a part of the Church, the Bride of Christ, the one that is still in the business of loving God and our neighbors. I know that when we are doing this, they will know we are His disciples.

Even as I have written this, I have been convicted by the things in my life that I know do not represent Jesus and my belief in Him in a positive light. I do not believe it is necessary for me to say to you specifically what that is or why I feel that way. But it is critically important that I admit it to Him that these things exist and that I turn from them and go forward changed.

The world can only know what we are showing them, and what we are showing them is all they see. Our lives, yours and mine, and the way we are living them, are what they are using to develop the perceptions they have of us as believers and of the Church in general. For many, this may very well be all that they will ever know of Jesus.

The question becomes, are we comfortable with what they are seeing?

You and I have been given such an awesome privilege, and we share in such an incredible honor when we realize that we are called to be His ambassadors: His representatives to our world. Much of the time we neglect to see this as our responsibility. My prayer is that we can become people who embrace this reality and then live lives that confirm it.

WHERE IS GOD IN HIS CHURCH?

He is right where we have placed Him, isn't He? Now we must decide whether we have placed Him in His rightful place. He must be the Head of the Church and the Lord of our lives. Our focus must be on Him, our service must be to Him, our authority must come from Him, and our desire must be to demonstrate to others the love He has for us and for them. If we can do this, He will be the center of our lives and the Shepherd of His Church, and they will know He is God.

I would like for us all to be able to say He is where He belongs, at the Head of His Church, and that we are committed to carrying out His Mission of reaching our world with the Good News of Jesus Christ. We are the Body, His Church, and we are alive, active, and committed to demonstrating to those around us the same love He has so graciously shown to us.

I am confident if we can do this, the perceptions driving the world to be critical of the Church will change, and the world will be able to see the Church as it should be. What will it be able to see? It will be able to see God in His Church, and when they can see that, they will be attracted to it, and the Lord will add to our numbers those who are being saved.

How will they know we are His disciples? Jesus gave us that answer in John 13:35 HCSB: "By this all people will know that you are My disciples, if you have love for one another.""

Amen!